The Ultimate Book of
FLOWERS

The Ultimate Book of
FLOWERS

Kathleen Patterson

THUNDER BAY
P·R·E·S·S

Published in the United States by
Thunder Bay Press
An imprint of the Advantage Publishers Group
5880 Oberlin Drive, Suite 400
San Diego, CA 92121-4794
http://www.advantagebooksonline.com

Produced by
Saraband, The Arthouse, 752–756 Argyle Street,
Glasgow G3 8UJ, Scotland

ISBN 1-57145-526-4

10 9 8 7 6 5 4 3 2 1

Library of Congress Cataloging-in-Publication Data available upon request.

Page 1: A delicate rose-red spider lily (*Lycoris radiata*) works magic in the late summer garden.

Page 2: A dazzling sunflower (*Helianthus*), with its raylike petals, follows the sun's path across the sky as the day passes.

Page 3: Boldly striped King's Chrysanthemums light up a fall garden in San Joaquin County, California.

Below: Exquisitely tinted bearded iris captured in a watercolor by Carolyn Fox.

Essential Precautions on the Use of Herbs and Edible Flowers
Use only the designated species described and illustrated in reliable specialty sources in the preparation of food or garnish: many garden and wayside flowers look alike and are poisonous. Use only flowers that have been grown organically (without the use of pesticides and fertilizers—including bonemeal—or any other chemical additives). Wash plant material carefully and ensure it is free of insects, dirt, or disease symptoms. People who suffer from allergies, asthma, or hay fever should not eat flowers at all, nor should they be served to young children or anyone potentially vulnerable to disease. Always exercise extreme caution and consult your physician before using herbal remedies. Neither the author nor the publisher can be held responsible for any adverse reactions to flowers and herbs described in this volume.

THIS BOOK IS DEDICATED TO
NORA AND HAROLD HAWORTH-MADEN

Contents

Whether it is the first snowdrop to pierce the frozen ground, a luscious rose received on Valentine's Day, or a vivid poppy punctuating a barren patch of wasteland, the sight of a flower lifts the heart. Yet our response to a perfect bloom reaches far beyond the purely visual. Both the humble daisy and the exotic orchid send a profound message to the human psyche.

At its most atavistic, the language of flowers communicates to us the joy and sadness of existence: of our birth and flowering, and ultimately of our death. The tightly wrapped buds of spring signal the promise of new life unfolding; a summer bloom at the height of its beauty floods us with *joie de vivre* and a golden glow of wellbeing; but as we see a vibrant specimen begin to fade and wither as winter approaches, we are touched by feelings of regret and melancholy. It is no coincidence that the human life span has been compared to the four seasons since ancient times, for the cycle of nature both mirrors and foretells our birth, maturity, decline, and inevitable death. This is one of the primary reasons why flowers speak to us on such a deeply instinctual level, for as we

watch them unfold their petals to reveal their breathtaking loveliness, we know that the moment of their greatest glory also heralds their death. No wonder that great thinkers, poets, and artists of every world age and culture have meditated on the ephemeral flower as a poignant symbol of the transience of human life.

The association between flowers and the rites that mark the passage of life endures to this day: we send flowers to celebrate the birth of babies and to commemorate birthdays and anniversaries, the milestones of aging. We wreath brides

Opposite: The common and botanical names of the passion flower (Passiflora) both refer to its status as a "crucifixion flower." Its stigma and styles resemble a cross and a crown of thorns.

Below: Because its form suggests female sexuality, in China the orchid symbolizes fertility, love, and beauty.

Above: *The lotus that was revered by the ancient Egyptians as a sacred symbol of Isis, of rebirth, and of divine light emerging from the murky waters of primeval chaos, can be equated with the exquisite water lily* (Nymphaea).

this meaning. *Scabiosa* (scabious), on the other hand, has been credited with the power to soothe skin irritations since ancient times, so its botanical name, a variant of the Latin verb "to itch," is apt. Floral names may also recall myths and legends, like *Achillea* (yarrow or milfoil), a plant with which the Greek hero Achilles was said to have healed his wounded warriors—and which was used for the same purpose on American Civil War battlefields. Perhaps most famous is *Narcissus*, named for the handsome Greek youth who became obsessed with his own reflection in a pool. Religious connotations are encapsulated in the names of many flowers, too, including *Lilium*, the Latin for "purity," a quality that is identified with the Virgin Mary.

This chapter explores the fascinating history of the evolution of floral vocabulary. We follow the thread from the vivid characterizations of antiquity through the medicinal concerns of the Middle Ages and the pioneering botanical spirit of the Enlightenment, to the sentimental apotheosis of Victorian times.

The Vocabulary of Spirituality

The tradition of memorializing a death with a funereal wreath stretches back over the millennia, the circular shape symbolizing eternity and the blooms, a living link between this world and the next. Asphodels (a lily, now identified with *Asphodelus*, from which the daffodil also derives its name), which were said to grow beside the Acheron, a river in the Greek underworld of Hades, were believed to exist in the worlds of both the living and the deceased. The ancient Egyptians, Greeks, and Romans all garlanded their dead with flowers to ease

with blossoms and, of course, we lay flowers on graves. Yet even in the depths of mourning, it is impossible not to feel momentarily uplifted by the sight of a snow-white lily, or to be comforted by its heady fragrance. Similarly, those who witnessed the blood-red poppies that sprang up amid the carnage of the World War I battlegrounds understood that life would go on. In the end, because flowers are life-affirming, they are also life-enhancing symbols of hope.

The language of flowers contains many subtle nuances and subtexts, not all of which are readily apparent. Besides expressing intangible emotional concepts, flowers often send us a direct message through names that communicate information about their appearance or properties. *Cypripedium*, for example, resembles a dainty shoe, and its botanical name is appropriately composed of one of the names of the Greek goddess Aphrodite (*Kypris*) and the word for slipper (*pedilon*); many of its common names—lady's slipper orchid, moccasin flower—reiterate

gradation
sắc thái

•delicately beautiful

a soft leather slipper or shoe

their passage to the afterlife and to express their belief that the soul of the departed would live on. The significance of this floral symbol of wish-fulfillment survives to this day in the amaranth (*Amaranthus*, or love-lies-bleeding), a favored funereal flower of Classical times: its name is an abbreviation of the Greek word *amarantos*, "everlasting."

The concept of flowers having triple symbolism as emblems of birth, death, and rebirth is illustrated by the ancient Egyptians' veneration of the lotus, or waterlily. Awed by the seemingly miraculous way in which this exquisite flower bloomed in the muddy waters of the Nile, unfolding its petals to welcome the Sun and closing them as dusk fell, they dedicated the lotus to their supreme goddess, Isis, who restored her murdered husband, Osiris, to life just long enough to conceive their son, Horus. Believing that the lotus united the underworld, which was presided over by Osiris, with the heavens, the realm of Horus, the lotus was revered as a sacred and magical flower that simultaneously represented death and darkness and rebirth and light. Another flower important to the ancient Egyptians was the iris, on account of its perceived resemblance to Osiris's divine scepter.

Although the botanical genus may differ, the lotus also holds a paramount place in many Eastern cultures, with an almost universal symbolism of the flowering of the cosmos from the waters of chaos. Hindus regard it as sacred to the gods Brahma, the creator, and Vishnu, the preserver, as well as to the benevolent goddess Lakshmi, or Padma. In Buddhist belief, certain flowers, including the sweet-scented champak (*Michelia champaca*) are honored by dedication to

Buddha, but none exceeds the lotus's importance—indeed, Buddha himself is often described as the "Jewel in the Lotus." Although artistic representations of lotuses in Indian and Chinese art are highly stylized, they are believed to depict the waterbean (*Nelumbo*), a flower credited with such mystical powers that it is equated with the chakras—centers of spiritual power within the human body—in Eastern disciplines including yoga. Described by the Chinese as the "golden flower of Taoism," in Islam it is one of the flowers that grows in paradise.

Some flowers have greater spiritual significance in the East than in the West. In China, certain flowers are representative of the seasons, the peony (*Paeonia*), heralding the spring; the lotus, summer; the chrysanthemum, fall; and any blossom that flourishes during the fourth season, winter. Along with the bamboo, orchid, and plum, the chrysanthemum is regarded as a

Below: *The common and botanical names of the jasmine or jessamine* (Jasminum) *are derived from* yasmin, *the Arabic name that the Persians gave this fragrant climbing plant.*

"noble plant" in Chinese belief and represents scholarly retirement. Introduced to Japan about AD 400 by Buddhist monks, the sixteen-petaled chrysanthemum was later adopted as the emblem of the Japanese emperors, its descriptive name (*Ki Ku*, "Sun") identifying it as the symbol of the land of the "Rising Sun." In China, however, it was the peony, with its varied, but always positive, significance, that was selected as the imperial flower.

Noting that *Helianthus annuus* both resembles the solar disk and turns its head to follow the Sun's passage through the sky, the Incas venerated the golden sunflower as an earthly incarnation of their Sun god. The Greeks, whose sunflower was the heliotrope (*Heliotropium*, "turn to Sun"), told of the nymph Clytie, who was spurned by the Sun god, Helios. Bereft, she continued to follow his course so closely that she finally turned into a

Below: The modern pink (Dianthus plumarius or D. chinensis) *is a hybrid of the perpetual flowering carnation and the old-fashioned pink. It is thought that the color pink was named after the flower's common name, which is derived from the Middle English verb* poinken, *denoting the distressing of fabric to give a similar appearance to the pink's ragged petals.*

sunflower. Many other floral names were bequeathed to us by the ancient Greeks, who cherished their native blooms as living links with the deities. Although they attributed the overall responsibility for flowers to the goddess Chloris ("green shoot"), they believed that she was assisted by her husband, Zephyr, who, as the god of the West wind, breathed life into blooms at springtime, and by the Sun god, Helios, whose rays encouraged flowers to grow. The Moon goddess, Artemis, played her part by sending dew to revive the plants by night. (The Romans, who adopted many aspects of Greek religious belief and culture, called Chloris "Flora," the name that is used today to describe flowers of all kinds.) A number of other names that we use today have their origins in ancient Greece. According to the myth of the anemone, or windflower, for example, Zephyr became so enamored of a lovely nymph named Anemone that the jealous Chloris transformed her into a flower; deserted by Zephyr, the lonely Anemone welcomed the attentions of Boreas, the god of the North wind, unfolding her petals to embrace him on his appearance in spring.

With the decline of the Roman Empire and the rise of Christianity, a number of flowers were endowed with new names and meanings, including *Anemone coronaria*. The former embodiment of the pagan nymph was now said to have sprung from the blood of Christ as it flowed to the foot of the cross on which He had been crucified. Several other blooms are also regarded as "crucifixion flowers." The clove pink or gillyflower (*Dianthus caryophyllus*), whose scent is reminiscent of cloves—which resemble nails—recalls the nails of execution on the cross. The evening primrose (*Oenothera*), passion flower (*Passiflora*), and American dogwood (*Cornus florida*) are also said to bear the marks of Christ's passion.

Yet it was to the mother of Christ that early Christians mainly dedicated flowers (after all, most civilizations have identified flowers with the feminine principle, and even today gifts of flowers are rarely made to men). Although the multitude of flowers whose common names start with the description "lady's"—like lady's mantle, *Alchemilla*—testify to the almost wholesale dedication of the floral world to "Our Lady," some stand out through their repeated depiction in Christian, especially Renaissance, art. One such is the rose (*Rosa*), once a flower of "profane" love through its links with the Greco-Roman goddess of sensual love, Aphrodite/Venus, but transformed by Christianity into an emblem of spiritual love whose personification was the Virgin Mary. Rosaries, the strings of beads used as an aid to prayer when petitioning the mother of God, derive their name from her designation as the "Mystical Rose" of heaven, but also from a more prosaic practice: many monasteries prepared oil from roses, and once the fragrance had been extracted, the spent petals were compacted into rosary beads. The red rose was a symbol of Christ, too, its crimson hue representing His blood and its thorns his suffering, as well as the crown of thorns.

Consecrated to the Madonna during the second century AD, the white lily (*Lilium candidum* is commonly known as the "Madonna lily") features prominently in artistic depictions of the Annunciation. Like the Virgin Mary, the lily has been described as "white without and gold within," although it was once deemed

necessary to render it more "virginal" by removing the golden sexual organs before it was brought into Christian churches to celebrate the Feast of the Annunciation (the term "gilding [gelding] the lily" attests to this practice). The adoption of the fleur-de-lys as the emblem of France may also have Christian origins, for it is said that the military victories of

Above: *Linnaeus named the* Iris *after the Greek goddess of the rainbow who acted as a messenger between the immortal and mortal realms. In the Victorian language of flowers, the iris denoted "a message."*

Below: *Although the columbine is associated with the Holy Spirit — symbolized by the dove — in Christian tradition, its botanical name, Aquilegia, is believed to be derived from either the Latin word for "eagle," aquila, or that denoting a water gatherer, aquilegus.*

Clovis (465–511), the Merovingian king of the Franks and the defender of the Christian faith against the Arian Visigoths, were due to his shield, on which three golden lilies were emblazoned on an azure ground. The story goes that an angel bearing this shield appeared before a pious hermit and told him to instruct Queen Clothilde to give it to her husband.

As well as being dedicated to the Madonna, the lily may also represent the Christian Trinity, or "three in one," as do the three-petaled iris and *Viola tricolor*, which was once known as herb trinity (*Herba trinitatis*). Because the *Aquilegia's* shape resembles a dove (and one of the flower's common names, columbine, is derived from the Latin word for dove, *columba*), it is an emblem of the Holy Spirit, stems being depicted with seven flowers signifying the Holy Spirit's seven gifts. Flowers of vivid blue were believed to enjoy the Virgin Mary's favor, too, because they mirrored the color of the mantle within which she protects and consoles the vulnerable. The bluebell (*Hyacinthoides*, or *Endymion nonscripta*) is one such flower, which, because it hangs its head, was thought to be in a state of perpetual grief for Christ's death, as was the snowdrop (*Galanthus*). Another "grieving flower" is the humble violet (*Viola odorata*): originally white, it was said to have adopted its hue of mourning in empathy with Mary's desolation.

The marigold, or "Mary's gold" (*Calendula officinalis*), is another of the Madonna's flowers, as is the cowslip (*Primula veris*), which was often called "Our Lady's Keys" because Mary plays an intercessory role between mortals and Christ and thus is credited with holding the keys to heaven. However, St. Peter is the official guardian of the gates to heaven, and legend said that he once dropped his keys to earth, thereby causing cowslips to blossom. As a result, they were variously called peterwort, peterkin, or herb Peter (and, in France, *clefs de Saint Pierre*). The list of flowers that have been dedicated to Christian saints is too long to enumerate; one, however, merits mention because its name is synonymous with its patron saint: *Veronica*.

The Vocabulary of Healing

Humanity has long been aware of the healing properties of certain flowers, shamans having practiced herbology since prehistoric times and herbal cures having been catalogued in such works as the Chinese *Pen T'Sao* (dating from around 2800 BC) and ancient Egypt's Ebers Papyrus (2000 BC). Even where such ancient knowledge was not recorded on papyrus or stone, it prevailed. For example, when tea became scarce in the American colonies after the Boston Tea Party of 1773, Native Americans of the Oswego tribe showed the rebellious colonists how to brew a fragrant, bergamot-scented tea from the monarda, or bee balm (*Monarda didyma*.)

Many ancient healing principles and practices espoused remarkably unified theories and treatments. Both traditional Chinese and Indian Ayurvedic medicine, for instance, concur with the theory of the humors (that the elements govern a person's health, and that any imbalance causes sickness), which originated in Europe with the ancient Greek "father of medicine," Hippocrates (468–377 BC), and advocate similar floral therapies. Hippocrates' teachings were amplified and popularized by the Greek physician Galen (AD 131–201) in *De Simplicibus*, an herbal that provided a valuable source of floral information to the Romans and later to the Arabs, who restored this forgotten knowledge to Europe as the Dark Ages drew to a close. Other highly influential classical herbals were *De Materia Medica*, dating from around AD 60, compiled by Pedanius Dioscorides, a Greek physician attached to the Roman Army, and *Naturalis Historia*, written by the Roman naturalist Pliny the Elder in AD 77.

Once these sources of ancient knowledge had been rediscovered at the start of the second millennium, Christian monks set about copying and disseminating them for the benefit of the sick whom they tended in their monasteries, plants being the only form of medication then available. The production of herbals was greatly accelerated by William Caxton's invention of the printing press in 1476, and during the sixteenth century the works of such authors as Nicholas Culpeper, John Parkinson, and John Gerard became much-consulted guides to the treatment of ailments with flowering plants. The sixteenth-century herbalists drew heavily upon the works of Hippocrates and Dioscorides (sometimes

Above: *When Leonhard Fuchs dubbed the foxglove Digitalis (from the Latin word for "finger," digitus) in 1542, he was echoing the many folk tales that told of fairies (popularly known as "folk," of which "fox" is a corruption) protecting their fingers with the flower's petals. The same practice was attributed to the Virgin Mary, which explains why the flower is also called (from "Our Lady") ladies' gloves or thimbles.*

Below: *As its name suggests, the rhizomes* [than the] *of the bloodroot (Sanguinaria), which originates from the American Northeast, ooze red-colored sap when damaged. Another of its common names,* [ed'zē'mūn] *puccoon, from a Native American language, recalls its traditional use as a pigment for body painting.*

erroneously, in their quest to identify the plants Dioscorides had observed in Asia Minor with natives of Europe), as well as upon a theory proposed by the famed Swiss alchemist Theophrastus of Bombastus, better known as Paracelsus (1493–1541). According to Paracelsus's Doctrine of Signatures, a plant's appearance clearly indicated the part of the body that it could treat. Hence because the mottled leaves of the *Pulmonaria* (from the Latin for lung, *pulmo*) resemble a human lung, the lungwort was believed to be effective in the treatment of pulmonary conditions. If they are damaged, blood-red sap flows from the roots of the *Sanguinaria* (*sanguis* means "blood" in

Latin), from which both Classical and medieval herbologists inferred that the bloodroot would cure any deficiency of the blood. As their names suggest, some plants were considered to be cure-alls: all heal (*Valeriana*, or valerian), for example, as well as angelica (*Archangelica officinalis*), *Potentilla* (whose name is derived from the Latin *potens*, "powerful," an indication of its efficacy), *Solidago* ("make whole"), and vervain (*Herba sacra*, the Romans' "sacred plant").

The achievements of modern medicine and pharmacology have meant that most traditional flower remedies have been dismissed and forgotten. Not all, however: the drug digitalin, for example, which regulates an erratic heartbeat, originated from the dried leaves of some species of foxglove, a plant that our ancestors imbued with both magical and healing powers. (However, *Digitalis purpurea*, the common foxglove, and other species are poisonous.) Drinking a cup of jasmine tea still soothes and refreshes the spirit, while the increasing popularity of such "alternative" therapies as aromatherapy, homeopathy, and flower remedies indicates that the belief in the healing power of flowers—whether physical or psychological—endures.

If a flower has historically been endowed with therapeutic properties, its name will signal this information. Any common name that includes the name of a body part is a near-infallible guide, as is the suffix "-wort," which is derived from the Old English word *wyrt*, meaning "root," another indicator of its therapeutic history. For instance, *Campanula latifolia*'s common name, throatwort, gives us insight into its past usage. The Latin designation *officinalis* in a flower's botanical name also reveals its traditional healing properties.

The Vocabulary of Science

From the seventeenth century, the study of flowering plants gradually began to move away from the realm of folklore to evolve into the scientific discipline of botany. A Reflection of the Age of Enlightenment's interest in science, plants were put under the microscope and their characteristics and properties observed and recorded. Following a process started by eminent emissaries to foreign climes, including Ogier Ghiselm de Busbecq, an ambassador of the Holy Roman Empire to the court of the Ottoman (Turkish) sultan Suleiman the Magnificent, who was the first to dispatch tulip bulbs to Europe in 1554, new species were discovered by intrepid botanical explorers. Some of them forfeited their lives in their obsessive mission to track down floral exotica in such far-flung regions as South America, Australia, and the Himalayas. An analysis of sixteenth-century herbals shows that the number of plant species that were recorded as growing in the British Isles was then about two hundred; by 1839 this number had rocketed to approximately eighteen thousand.

This extraordinary influx of botanical species created a nightmare of nomenclature that was eventually resolved by the Swedish botanist and physician Carl von Linné, or Linnaeus (the Latin form of his name). Until the introduction of Linnaeus's binomial ("two name") system in 1735, botanists had to conform to the convention of precisely listing the features of a plant's appearance—petals, stalk, leaves, and all—in Latin to ensure that their peers would understand which plant they were referring to. Nor did it help that the same common name was frequently used to describe different plants

(even today, the strawflower may denote *Helichrysum* or *Bracteantha*). Linnaeus's achievement was to devise a simple system by which a plant bore two names: that of its genus and that of its species, both typically made up of either Latin or Greek roots. Because the traditional language of science and medicine was Latin, and because both Latin and Greek were universally used by members of the scientific community, whatever their nationality, the new botanical language could be understood the world over.

Above: *Because its stems are hollow, the botanical name of the lilac is* Syringa, *after the Greek word* syrinx, *"pipe." Prior to its introduction to Europe, the Ottoman Turks fashioned pipes from the lilac, and its common name is derived from the Arabic word for the color blue,* laylak.

Above: The aroma exuded by the flowers of the Roman chamomile, or camomile (Chaemaemelum nobilis), was compared by both the ancient Greeks and the Spanish to the smell of apples, hence its Greek designation khamaimelon, "ground apple," and its Spanish name manzanilla, "little apple."

According to Linnaeus's full system, a plant's classification comprises its division, class, subclass, order, family, genus, and species. In practice, however, a flower's name is generally abbreviated to its genus and species, so that an oriental poppy, for instance, is designated *Papaver* (poppy) *orientale* (oriental). The species name pinpoints any of a number of notable features, including the flower's appearance (*pallidus* or *pallida*, for example, meaning pale-colored), qualities (*odoratus* or *odorata* signifying scented, and *hirsutus* or *hirsuta*, hairy), season of flowering (*vernus* or *verna* identifying spring), habitat (*maritimus* or *maritima* signaling a coastal plant), and country of origin (*sinensis* or *sinensa* denoting China). When a new plant is identified, its discoverer publishes its name and details in a botan-

ical journal, and many have chosen to honor distinguished individuals in this way. Dr. Gronovius, for example, paid homage to his contemporary Linnaeus by naming the twinflower *Linnaea borealis*. Other individuals whose names have thus been immortalized include Michael Bégon, the patron of Charles Plumier, who named the begonia for him, and explorer Captain Meriwether Lewis, the namesake of the lewisia, who crossed America overland with William Clark.

Besides creating an international language of flowers, Linnaeus instituted an evocative floral vocabulary that is as accurate as it is intriguing. If you had never seen a forget-me-not, for instance, but had a smattering of Latin and Greek, you could correctly surmise from its botanical name alone that the *Myosotis* (from the Greek *mus*, "mouse" and *otis*, "ear") has mouse-shaped leaves.

The Vocabulary of Love

Flowers have always played a pivotal part in the language of love, forget-me-nots and roses having long been especially favored by lovers. According to a medieval legend, the forget-me-not was named by a German knight who drowned while stooping to pick the diminutive flower for his lady, and whose dying words were *Vergiß mich nicht* ("Forget me not"). Roses were originally sacred to the classical love goddess Aphrodite, or Venus, and their amorous message is retained to this day in the practice of presenting red roses to a loved one, particularly on Valentine's Day. During the Middle Ages, knights would pin daisies (*Bellis perennis*) to their armor to signal their fidelity in love, and young girls still hopefully chant "He loves me, he loves me not" while plucking the petals one by one from the "day's eye" flower.

Although these associations have existed for centuries, it was the Victorians who elevated the sentimental language of flowers to unprecedented heights. It is said that when Lady Mary Wortley Montagu, the wife of the English ambassador to the Ottoman Empire, arrived in Istanbul in the early eighteenth century, she was captivated by the practice whereby the ladies of the harem sent each other coded messages in floral form. On her return to England, Lady Mary published a floral vocabulary based on her observations. John Huddlestone Wynne's *Fables of Flowers* followed in 1775, succeeded by such widely read floral dictionaries as Charlotte de la Tour's *Le Langage des Fleurs* (1819) and Thomas Miller's *The Poetical Life of Flowers* (1847). Robert Tyas's *The Handy Book of the Language of Flowers* (1864) was reprinted an astonishing 13,000 times, American works, like Mrs. E. Washington Wirt's *Flora's Dictionary*, enjoying similar popularity. Inspired by such guides, the Victorians developed a mania for floral communication, sending each other carefully collated bouquets and holding "floral-conversation" evenings to practice and improve their proficiency in the language of flowers.

Although the Victorians allowed many flowers to retain their traditional meanings—the *Viola odorata*, or sweet violet, for example, still signified modesty—others took on a more convoluted significance, like the Japan rose (*Rosa japonica*), which declared sternly that "Beauty is your only attraction." While most flowers sent flattering messages of love, coquetry, and admiration, if you received a posy consisting of begonia, wild ranunculus, and

belvedere blooms, your heart would have been chilled by the realization that someone harbored "dark thoughts" about "ingratitude," causing them to "declare against you." If you were of a charitable disposition, you may have responded with a placatory mixture of gentians ("you are unjust"), nemophila (but "I forgive you") and valerian (because "I have an accommodating spirit").

It is a sad fact that most of us today are floral illiterates, little dreaming of the wealth of mythological, spiritual, historical, herbal, botanical, and sentimental associations that a single bloom can convey. Yet does our ignorance really matter, when the mere sight of a flower in bloom has the power instantly to cheer us? Perhaps its unspoken affirmation of the beauty of life is the most important message of all.

Below: In Hindu belief, jasmine (Jasminum) *is so prized for its exquisite beauty and fragrance that the "queen of the night," as it is called, is sacred to the god Vishnu. Early Christians compared the shape of its tiny white blooms with heavenly stars and hence dedicated the jasmine to the Virgin Mary.*

Lys Rouge

Le Lys rouge, ou orange est une espece de Narcisse, qui a   lsignon, les feuilles et la tige presque toutes
semblable; Il porte au haut de sa tige cinq ou Six belles fleurs   comme des petites tulipes de couleur orangé,
pâle, a fond blanc par dedans; les feuilles de celuy cy sont beaucup   plus minces et plus delicates que celles de nos
tulipes; Ils ont cinq petits filets a languettes jaunes, Mais Ils non   point de bouton, comme la tulipe; cette fleur
est fort belle, Mais elle na point d'odeur,

Botanical Illustrations

As exquisite as these drawings are, their creators did not intend them to be works of art per se, but rather a means of disseminating botanical knowledge through the accurate depiction of their floral subjects.

At left is *Lys rouge* ("red lily," *Lilio-narcissus purpureus*), a watercolor by Charles Plumier (1646–1704) that was published in his botanical catalog *Plantes de la Martinique et de la Guadeloupe* in 1688.

Commissioned by the Empress Josephine in 1798 to translate the living beauty of her gardens at Château Malmaison into art, the French botanical artist Pierre Joseph Redouté (1759–1840) won acclaim in his own lifetime for the delicacy of his stipple-engraved aquatints. Redouté's exquisite rendition of an orchid is illustrated on page 23, and on the opposite page is Langlois's homage to the master illustrator, a depiction of the *Rosa indica subviolacea* that appeared in Redouté's volume of rose illustrations, *Les Roses*.

Rosa Indica subviolacea   *Rosier des Indes a fleurs presque violettes*

P. J. Redouté pinx   Imprimerie de Remond   Langlois sculp

Spice of Life *Overleaf*

Johan Michael Seligmann's depiction of a saffron crocus (*Crocus sativus*, page 22) first appeared in Germany in 1750. As well as being valued for the color and flavoring that it imparted to food, this most ancient of crocuses was also believed to have medicinal properties.

Arts and Flowers

Native to Africa and Asia, the *Thunbergia harrisii* (above) is depicted here in an illustration published in Germany in 1861. Two centuries earlier, when Nicolas Robert immortalized this trio of tulips (*Tulipa*) in watercolor, Europe had only recently emerged from the feverish period of "tulipomania."

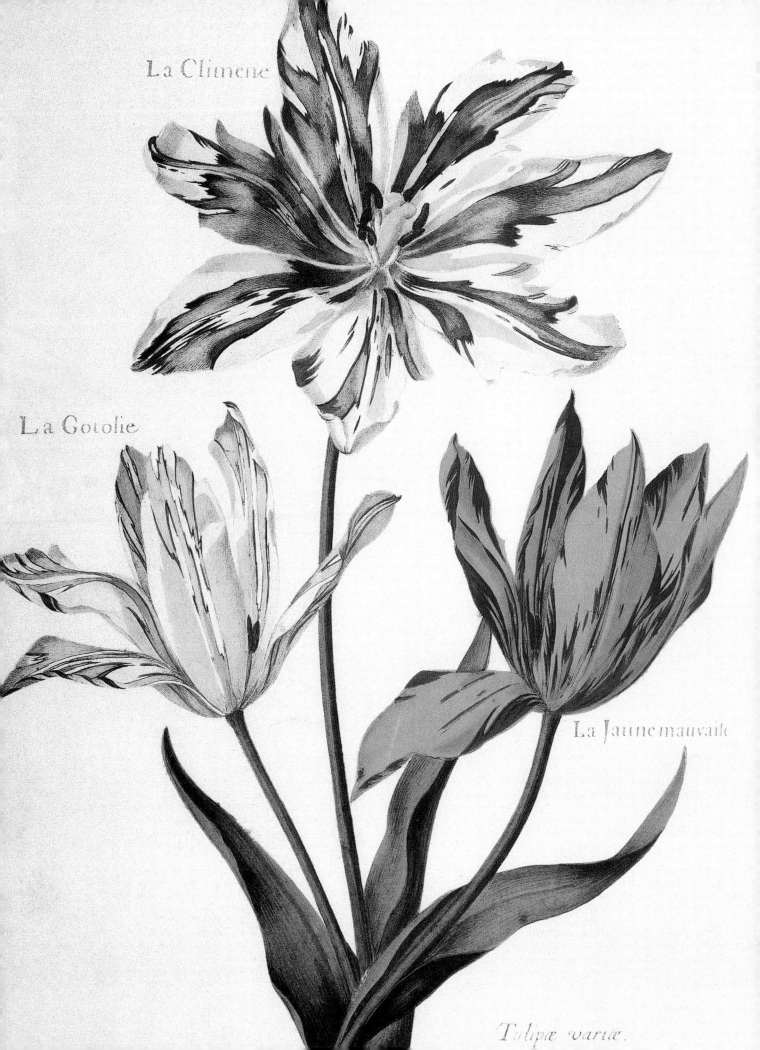

La Climene

La Gotolie

La Jaune mauvaise

Tulipæ variæ.

the true Saffron.

Cheerful Blooms of Spring

The crocus's name comes from the Greek *krokos*, "saffron": the fall-flowering saffron crocus is *Crocus sativus*, whose dried stigmas have been used to flavor food and produce an orange pigment for millennia. Today, however, the more popular crocuses are the decorative, spring-flowering varieties, such as the *Crocus sieberi* "Firefly," shown above.

Another much-loved spring flower is the tulip (*Tulipa*), opposite, which is so common today that it is hard to believe that the purchase of a single bulb bankrupted many Dutch enthusiasts during the "tulipomania" of the seventeenth century. The flower is now regarded as the national bloom of The Netherlands.

Observers of the Sun

Despite their strong resemblance to common daisies, the members of the *Leucanthemum* family (opposite: *L. vulgare*; above: *L. x superbum*, the Shasta daisy) actually belong to the *Chrysanthemum* genus, the true daisy being *Bellis perennis*. The etymology of the word "daisy" can be traced back to the Old English *daeges eaye*, or "day's eye," which describes the flower's habit of unfurling its petals in response to the Sun's rays.

[handwritten annotation: giương, phất, mở trải]

Flowers of Innocence *Overleaf*

Wherever they grow, be it on a mountain pasture, as here, with the stunning backdrop of the Grand Tetons, or in a city garden, daisies and flowers of related families or similar appearance, like balsamroot and balm, are always associated with innocence and an unspoiled nature. Children adore making daisy chains, and in folklore it is said that a child wearing a wreath of daisies is protected from abduction by fairies.

Life and Death *Overleaf*

Although the chrysanthemum is a symbol of longevity in China, since its introduction to Europe in 1789, this fall-flowering bloom has become linked with death in the Western mind through its portent of winter and its widespread association with mourning and funerals. Indeed, in Italy it is known as "the flower of death," *Fiori dei Morte*.

The Flower of Enchantment

The lily (*Lilium,* right) has been admired since ancient times, and many mythical figures have been associated with it over the millennia. A charming English folk belief holds that when a lily seed germinates, an elf is born as its companion.

A Sophisticated Beauty

Distinctive and delicate, orchids (*Orchis;* below, the oxblood orchid) are universally associated with elegance and beauty, as celebrated in the work of Decadent (Aesthetic-movement) artists like Aubrey Beardsley (1872–98).

A Strategy for Attraction

The orchid family, *Orchidaceae*, comprises more than 20,000 species, including *Phelaenopsis x* "Carmela's Stripe" (above). Many flowers within this family have evolved specifically to resemble, and hence attract, the insects that pollinate them.

Emblem of Scotland *Page 34*

The thistle, the national flower of Scotland, signifies austerity in the Victorian language of flowers. The milk thistle pictured here (*Silybum marianum*), as well as the blessed thistle (*Carduus benedictus*), were once believed to help nursing mothers to produce more milk.

Filled with the Joys of Spring

In the Victorian language of flowers, the spring-flowering crocus (opposite) signifies youthful gladness, an appropriate description for one of the first flowers to burst into exuberant life after the barren winter months.

A Pensive Look *Overleaf*

Because its bowed head gives it a contemplative appearance, one of the common names of the various *Viola* cultivars, pansy, is derived from the French verb *penser*, "to think." Thoughtfulness was also the message signified by the pansy in Victorian times.

The Wearer of Different Hats *Page 35*

The *Aquilegia*'s many common names include columbine and granny's bonnet. The flower's appearance has also been compared with that of a jester's cap, which is probably why this flower was associated with folly and whimsy in the Victorian language of flowers.

The Regalia of Divinity *Page 39*

The iris was associated with Osiris, the ancient Egyptian god of the underworld, largely because the bloom resembled the shape of his scepter, which was the symbol of his divine authority.

Hearts and Lockets

It is easy to see why one of the common names of *Dicentra spectabilis* (right) is "bleeding heart." Its alternative designations, "ladies' lockets" and "Dutchman's breeches," are equally evocative, while if you prize open the flower slightly, you may well see a "lady in the bath," another of its popular names.

Lovers Entwined

Linnaeus bestowed the botanical name *Lonicera* on the honeysuckle (below) in 1753, thereby honoring Adam Lonitzer, or Lonicer, a sixteenth-century German botanist. The name "honeysuckle" refers to the nectar's honeylike taste, while its habit of twining itself tightly around a host plant has earned it the name woodbind, or woodbine, and caused it to be likened to a lover who clings to her sweetheart.

Sun Worshippers *Overleaf*

A field of golden sunflowers (*Helianthus annuus*) follows the Sun's path across the sky. Native to South America, these huge flowers were originally prized more for the oil that is extracted from their seeds than for their spectacular beauty.

A Heady Fragrance

The intensely perfumed frangipani (*Plumeria rubra*, left), which is native to the American tropics, is named for the sixteenth-century Italian marquis Muzio Frangipane, who invented a method of imbuing gloves with a scent extracted from *Iris florentina*. Here, the fragrant flowers are arranged as an offering for a sacred ritual in Ubud, Bali.

Art Imitates Life

Water lilies like the one below (*Nymphaea*, for the Greek water nymph, Nymphe), which grew in the famous water gardens at Giverny, inspired the celebrated *Nymphéas* series by the French Impressionist artist Claude Monet (1840–1926).

Jewels of Nature

A blazing field of Indian blanket flowers (*Gaillardia*, opposite) brings to mind the poetic words of George Croly (1780–1860): "The flowers are nature's jewels, with whose wealth she decks her summer beauty."

A Sacred Offering

The brilliant hibiscus (above), the state flower of Hawaii, flourishes in tropical climates. Signifying sacred love and beauty in many Eastern cultures, it is often used to garland the images of divine entities, as in this scene on the Indonesian island of Bali.

By Any Other Name

As its name suggests, the hybrid tea rose "Christian Dior" (above) was first bred during the twentieth century—one of the countless varieties of *Rosa* (Latin for "red") that have been cultivated and cherished over the millennia as emblems of romantic love.

Symbols of Death and Rebirth

The narcotic qualities of opium have caused poppy varieties like *Papaver somniferum* ("the poppy that brings sleep," opposite) to become associated with death, yet because they self-seed so prolifically, poppies are also a symbol of hope and rebirth.

Love, Not War *Page 54*

The red rose generally signifies sensual love, and the white rose, <u>chastity</u>. But during the English civil wars of 1455–85—the Wars of the Roses—the red rose (*Rosa provincialis*) and the white rose (*R. alba*) represented the rival houses of Lancaster and York, respectively. The two varieties were crossbred to celebrate the political marriage of Henry Tudor and Elizabeth of York in 1486, thereby creating the Tudor rose.

Of Moon and Sun *Page 55*

The fragrant white moonflower, pictured here, and the morning glory belong to the same genus, *Ipomoea*. The primary difference between them is that the evocatively named moonflower's blooms open at night to perfume the summer air, while the morning glory's flowers open after sunrise and last only one day.

Everlasting

The colorful strawflower (*Helichrysum*, above) gained its common name of "everlasting" because its papery bracts are so long-lasting when dried, giving these garden favorites year-round appeal.

One for the Pot

The pot marigold opposite (*Calendula officinalis*) is so called because enterprising medieval cooks, who could not afford expensive saffron, used it to give a golden hue and subtle flavor to their dishes.

Mythical Blooms of the Underworld

Overleaf

The wild <u>daffodils</u> (*Narcissus pseudonarcissus*) that so captivated the poet William Wordsworth (1770–1850) were once regarded as funereal flowers, such "affodils" being equated with the <u>asphodels</u> that were said to grow in the ancient Greek underworld, Hades. Vivid and cheerful enough to offset the chill of the season, it is hard to imagine these bright heralds of spring in such a context.

A Jealous Beauty

The yellow rose, opposite, which was imported to Europe from Persia during the sixteenth century, represented jealousy in the Victorian language of flowers. Today, it is widely used as an emblem of <u>friendship</u> and <u>remembrance.</u>

In Loving Memory

The Latin name of the <u>primrose,</u> above, *Primula vulgaris* (*vulgaris* meaning "common"), is derived from its former designation as the "first rose of spring," *prima rosa* ("rose" in this sense denoting any beautiful flower). In <u>Roman legend,</u> the divine couple Priapus and Flora created it to commemorate their son Paralysus, who <u>pined away</u> following the death of his sweetheart, Melicentra.

More Haste, Less Speed

The *Impatiens* (Latin for "impatient"), or Busy Lizzie, pictured below, gained its botanical name from the speed with which it ejects its seeds from their pods, which Charles Darwin's grandfather, Erasmus Darwin (1731–1802), compared to "hurl[ing] her infants from her frantic arms."

A Floral Insignia

The name *Gladiolus* (from the Latin *gladius*, "gladiator's sword") aptly describes the pointed shape of this plant's leaves (opposite); in medieval times it was also known as "sword-flag." The nickname "glads" suggests the uplifting brightness of its colorful blooms.

A Protective Amulet bùa hộ mạng

The ancient Greek poet Homer, in his epic the *Iliad*, tells us that the peony (*Paeonia,* opposite) was named for Paeon, the physician who used its root to heal the wounds sustained by the gods during the Trojan War. Both roots and seeds were once believed to protect against evil, as well as many physical and mental afflictions.

Crowning Glories

Along with carnations and Sweet Williams, pinks (below) belong to the *Dianthus* family, whose name is a Latinized composite of the Greek words *dios,* "divine," and *anthos,* "flower." *Dianthus* blooms were woven into the wreaths worn during Greco-Roman religious festivals, and it is believed that "carnation" is a corruption of "coronation."

cẩm chướng , adj(hồng nhạt) lễ lên ngôi , lễ đăng quang

"Joyful Newes"

One of the common names of the *Monarda didyma* (above), bee balm, describes the magnetic attraction that its flowers exert on bees. The *Monarda* was named for Nicolas Monardes (1493–1588), a Spanish physician whose botanical work *Joyfull Newes out of the Newe Founde Worlde* was published in 1569; Monardes himself called the plant that was later named for him "berg-amot." In the United States, *Monarda didyma* is often called Oswego tea, in recognition of the tisane that members of the Oswego tribe taught the colonists to brew when tea imported from Britain was boycotted.

From the Holy Land

We can only speculate that the prefix "holly" in "holly-hock" (opposite) once meant "holy" because the plant was introduced to England by the Crusaders from the Holy Land. Alternatively, it may have been used to reduce swelling in horses' hocks: both the hollyhock and its relative in the *Alcea* family, the mallow, were once considered cure-alls.

A Nosegay of Names

[bó hoa thơm]

The *Antirrhinum* (opposite) is most commonly known as the snapdragon *[hoa mõm chó]*, but its alternative name, calf's snout, also reflects the etymology of the genus name, which means "noselike."

A Goddess Among Roses

According to Hindu myth, the god Vishnu created his consort, *[vợ]* Lakshmi, the goddess of beauty and prosperity, from 108 rose petals, and embellished her with ten times that number. *[làm đẹp, trang điểm, thêm]*

65

"In Flanders' Fields..." *Previous Pages*

Poppies, once said to spring from the blood of fallen soldiers, have become a poignant symbol of the slaughter of World War I, immortalized in the opening lines of John McCrae's poem: "In Flanders' fields the poppies grow/Between the crosses row on row …."

Turban Trim

The name of the tulip (*Tulipa*, right) comes from the Arabic word for a man's turban, *tulipant*, whose shape it resembles and to which the flower was often pinned as an adornment.

Salad Days *Overleaf*

The vigorous, easy-to-grow nasturtium (*Tropaeolum*) got its unflattering Latin name because inhaling its peppery fragrance causes the nose (*nasus*) to wrinkle or twist (*tortus*). In fact, both the tangy leaves and the flowers are popular in salads and garnishes.

Here Be Dragons *Page 71*

Generations of childen have made a summer pastime of gently squeezing the sides of the snapdragon flower (*Antirrhinum*) to make the "dragon" snap open its mouth and stick out its "tongue."

Garden Flowers and Wildflowers

There are many reasons why people first began to cultivate flowers and create gardens. They may have wanted a ready supply of floral remedies, or of fragrances with which to scent their bodies, clothing, or homes, or they may simply have been captivated by the beauty of the flowering plants that they saw growing wild. Indeed, all garden flowers were originally wildflowers that the early gardener wished to "capture" and grow in his or her own garden—a motivation that has not changed over the millennia.

Although we now usually grow flowering plants for their loveliness alone, this was not always the case: some were once especially prized for their nutritional value, including American natives like the sunflower (*Helianthus annuus*) and the dahlia. Another important aspect of the evolution of the garden flower is importation: it is believed that the Romans were responsible for introducing a number of non-native plants to the countries that they conquered. This served partly to provide their citizens in exile with familiar fruits, (for example, by introducing the fig, *Ficus carica*, to Britain) or their

medicinal herbs (like the valerian, *Valeriana officinalis*), and partly to provide the invaders with the solace of the sight and smell of flora that reminded them of home. And during the latter half of the second millennium, scores of botanists scoured the world for floral exotica that they later introduced to their homelands, where they subsequently became naturalized. Nowadays, however, you need look no farther than a horticultural catalogue or your local nursery to obtain virtually any plant that appeals to you.

Garden flowers of the same genus as their wild relatives often look very different—this is because successive horticulturists have followed a process of selective breeding, by which the most vigorous, loveliest, or sweetest-smelling flowering plants have been propagated, while wildflowers have been left to their own devices. And although their reproductive cycle was not properly understood until the eighteenth century, early horticulturists knew very well how to increase their stock by gathering seeds, taking cuttings, and dividing roots. In addition, crossbreeding, or hybridization, has produced types of flowers that do not exist in the wild. One

Opposite: *Rhododendrons will reward you with spectacular blooms like this only if you establish them in acid soil. Being alkaline- or lime-hating members of the* Ericaceae *family, they will decline if the soil's pH value is more than 7.0.*

73

Right: *Woody goldenrod*
(Chrysoma
pauciflosculosa)
flourishes in the dunes of
Mississippi's Gulf Islands
National Seashore.

of the most spectacular results of such hybridization is the hybrid tea rose *La France,* which first appeared in 1867, a cross between the tea rose that was introduced to Britain in 1810 and the hybrid perpetual that was first bred in 1837.

Even though all manner of flowering plants are widely sold by nurseries today, you only need some basic knowledge and a few tools and materials to increase your stock, and the satisfaction gained from watching a flowering plant that you have

"created" grow and flourish is immense. It is small wonder that gardening arouses such passion in those who have been bitten by the horticultural bug. Although the temptation to uproot a particularly attractive wildflower from its natural habitat—be it wasteland, woodland, grassland, mountain, meadow, coast, or wetland—so that you can transplant it into your own garden may seem overwhelming, don't succumb. Not only are many wildflowers now protected by law, but by removing them you may inadvertently cause irreparable damage to the environment and food chain. In any case, most wildflower varieties are now sold either as seeds or as young plants.

Whether it be a butterfly's paradise, an old-fashioned cottage garden, or a haven that reflects your own unique style, this chapter aims to guide and inspire you to create your ideal garden. Through a few judicious choices from the wealth of flowering plants of every hue, fragrance, and habit, you can design a magical, ever-changing tapestry of color, texture, and form.

The Faithful Perennial and Ephemeral Annual

The perennial is the gardener's faithful friend, for, unlike the annual, which flowers in the year of seeding and then dies, or the biennial, which lives for only two years, it will survive for many years. By building a living armature of trees, shrubs, and flowering perennials, you will be rewarded by an enduring garden that you can also fill out and vary from year to year by planting annuals and biennials.

Perennials comprise a number of categories, including evergreen perennials; deciduous, or border, perennials (whose foliage usually dies back in winter); rockery perennials (the diminutive alpine, desert, or coastal plants); tender perennials (which have to be protected from frost); wetland, or bog, plants (which require humus-rich, damp soil); and bulbous plants. This may seem a short list until you realize that not only does each component contain hundreds of different genera and species, but that they offer the imaginative gardener boundless long-term possibilities in terms

of seasonal flowering, color and scent of blooms, shape and texture of leaves, as well as height and form.

They may be short-lived, but annuals bring such intense excitement and vividness of color to the horticultural picture that few gardeners would choose to be without them. Perhaps the essence of their attraction lies in their very ephemerality. Would a summer display be complete without a long-anticipated crop of golden marigolds (*Tagetes*), for example, or the lush proliferation of blooms of the poor man's orchid (*Schizanthus*)? Annuals also give you the opportunity to experiment, their advantage being that if the effect achieved is not to your liking, it will last only as long as the flowering season.

Below: Many people only consider that spring has truly arrived when their gardens are awash with daffodils (Narcissus cultivars). For the most striking effect, mass daffodil bulbs together at planting time.

Above: The common snowdrop (Galanthus nivalis) *is a bulbous hardy perennial that blooms from late winter to early spring, sometimes even bravely pushing its way through a blanket of snow.*

Choosing Flowers for Each Season

One of the primary planning concerns is ensuring that the garden will provide year-round color, not only to lift the spirits as each season gives way to the next, but also to provide continuous floral displays for the house. With the help of a good horticultural guide, a little patience, and some inevitable trial and error, you can create a garden that gladdens your heart and offers interest from spring through the winter months.

Spring blooms are inevitably the most eagerly awaited, each delicate flower being cherished as a welcome flash of life as the dreariness of winter gives way to the brighter skies of spring. This is when bulbous perennials come into their own. Among the first to appear are the hardy cyclamen (*Cyclamen coum*), the multihued crocus (*Crocus chrysanthus*), and the pearl-white snowdrop (*Galanthus nivalis*), all taking their places alongside such well-loved perennials as the Christmas rose (*Hellebore niger*). These early bloomers are followed by a crop of spring favorites, including a host of daffodils and narcissi (*Narcissus* cultivars), an ocean of Dutch hyacinths (*Hyacinthus orientalis* cultivars), a parade of jewel-bright, turban-headed tulips (*Tulipa* cultivars), in addition to the cheerful members of the primula family: primroses (*Primula vulgaris* and hybrids), cowslips (*Primula veris*), and polyanthus (*Primula variabilis*).

As spring blossoms into summer, so ever-increasing numbers of blooms burst into being. Perhaps the flower most closely associated with the season of nature's fruition is the rose, which delights gardeners almost as much as it does aphids. The rich variety of blooms that keep the queen of flowers company during the summer season are too numerous to list, but some of the notables include the bold-colored poppies (*Papaver* and *Meconopsis*), the richly petaled peonies (*Paeonia*) and the elegant irises and columbines (*Aquilegia vulgaris*), along with the pinks and carnations of the *Dianthus* family.

Almost imperceptibly, summer gives way to fall, when nature sends us warm-hued flowers as a consolation for the prospect of the winter ahead. This is when the ice plant (*Sedum spectabile*) rewards the gardener at last with the glorious sight of its pincushion of tiny pink or red flowers, when the New England aster or Michaelmas daisy (*Aster novae-angliae*) puts on a display of starbursts, and when the so-called obedient plant (*Physostegia* or *Dracocephalum virginiana*) obligingly lives up to its name.

Sadly, these late flowerers soon become a distant memory as the days grow shorter and the season begins to turn. Yet against the relatively bare backdrop of the winter garden, you may still see a few hardy flowers blooming bravely, including the winter pansy (*Viola* x *wittrockiana*) and the glory of the snow (*Chionodoxa*). And in only a few months, the cycle of the seasons will begin afresh.

Companionable Plantings: Color and Form

Although the sight of any flower is heartwarming, you will probably want to cultivate a garden of flowering plants that are not only individually pleasing, but also meld into a harmonious symphony of color, texture, and form.

When planning your garden, take the seasons into consideration to ensure that you will always be able to enjoy a splash of color, even in the depths of winter. For this reason, too, it is advisable to plant some winter-hardy evergreen shrubs at the edges of your garden, which will provide a permanently green canvas on which you can paint in the seasonal detail from a rich palette of floral shades. The bare bones of your garden are essentially its structural components: boundaries, lawn, and trees, patios and paths, as well

Below: *Few people can resist the simple charm of the numerous flowers that resemble the perennial daisy* (Bellis perennis).

as borders and beds. Some you will be able to alter or introduce, but others may well be permanent fixtures that you will have to work around. Other important factors that may influence how your garden will look are the types of flowering plant that you wish to establish, the prevailing climate, the predominance of sun or shade, and the soil type: clearly, the delicate blooms of tropical climes will not survive a Northern winter; a sun-seeking plant will die a slow death in the shade; nor will an acid-loving plant thrive in alkaline soil. Once you have determined the parameters within which you must

Below: *One effective way to highlight the vibrant golden color of marigolds is to plant them alongside flowers of other hues.*

work, you can let your imagination run riot. Remember that there are no rules when it comes to garden style: if it works, and you like it, anything goes. That having been said, there are a few guidelines regarding color and form that may help to provide inspiration for the flower lover.

In common with interior designers, when planning their outdoor rooms, many gardeners consult a color wheel on which the spectrum of color is arranged to help them visualize how the hue of one plant will complement another. Many garden designers suggest that the most stunning effects can be achieved by picking flowers that are either adjacent to, or opposite, each other on the color wheel, but let your own eye and your individual taste be your guide. It may be that you wish to focus on a single shade, or to create an elegant vista of whites and pastels. Perhaps you would prefer to electrify your garden with a brilliant mass of fuchsia pinks and scarlets. Alternatively, your preference may be for a calming mixture of blue and white blooms, or an energizing combination of sunny orange or yellow flowers. Remember, though, that a concentration of just a few shades, whether they be opposites, such as orange and blue, or related, like pink and red, can have a greater impact than a number of different-colored blooms. You can also maximize your chosen color effect by planting flowering plants in blocks and drifts rather than spacing them at wide intervals.

Regarding form, there are two aspects to consider: first, the overall form of your garden, and, second, the forms of the individual plants that will grow in it. If you are aiming to create a flat, desertlike vista, then you will probably opt for plants of the same diminutive height. If, on the

other hand, you prefer a perspective that gives the illusion of depth, you may prefer to site tall-growing shrubs at the back of your canvas, or maybe a trellis, up which a clematis, honeysuckle, jasmine, or rambling rose can wend its way, with medium-height flowering plants before them, and dwarf varieties or ground-hugging species at the front to soften the border's edges. Giving some thought to the form, texture, and color of foliage will also pay great dividends, especially during the fall and winter months. The burning bush or summer cypress (*Bassia scoparia,* f. *trichophylla*), for instance, with its dense, vivid green leaves that turn reddish-purple in fall, provides a fascinating focal point in itself and also acts as a striking foil to any adjacent, brightly hued summer flowers. To give another example, not only does the Japanese anemone (*Anemone hybrida*) bear beautiful flowers from late summer to mid-fall, but for the rest of the year its glossy, trifoliate, dark-green leaves provide a lush backdrop to its earlier-flowering neighbors. And then, there are many ornamental grasses…The combinations and permutations that are available to the imaginative gardener are literally endless.

Themed Gardens

When planning your garden, you may be inspired by a particular theme: perhaps a garden style of the past like the cottage garden; an alpine rockery filled with miniature floral treasures; an environmentally friendly haven that attracts butterflies and bees; or a wildflower meadow that brings the freshness of nature right to your own back door.

The picturesque Victorian cottage-style garden has become popular again, due to its fantastic mixture of flowers and herbs, as well as its unstructured charm. In the past, because cottagers were usually of

Above: The flowering plants that we commonly refer to as "marigolds" can belong to one of two genera (Calendula or Tagetes). All are distinguished by their cheerful sunny hues.

Above: Not only are foxgloves (Digitalis) *among the traditional staples of the cottage garden, but with their typical height of at least 3 feet (1 meter), they offer an eye-catching way of adding depth to a garden's color scheme. It should be remembered, though, that foxgloves are poisonous.*

modest means, they crammed their small plots with fruit-bearing trees, vegetables, and herbs for household consumption, as well as with sweet-smelling, inexpensive flowers that would refresh a weary soul after a hard day's work. Although today's cottage garden is essentially ornamental, it should appear as informal and as packed with life as its working predecessor. It should also contain some of the traditional blooms that were cottage-garden staples during the nineteenth century. Aim to include robust flowering plants that offer maximum color, vigor, and fragrance, like rambling roses, lavender, and honeysuckles (*Lonicera*), along with your personal favorites from an inexhaustible list that includes bleeding hearts (*Dicentra*), snapdragons (*Antirrhinum*), hollyhocks (*Alcaea*),

foxgloves (*Digitalis*), delphiniums, red hot poker (*Kniphofia*), sweet peas (*Lathyrus*), stock (*Matthiola*), wallflowers (*Cheiranthus*), larkspur (*Consolida*), and the pinks and carnations of the *Dianthus* family.

Most gardens attract insects and birds—be they welcomed or cursed—but if you include some specific flowering plants you will be assured of a host of summer visitors (note: remember to avoid the use of pesticides). If you wish to indulge your local bees, as well as many butterflies, try planting calamint (*Calamintha*), hyssop (*Hyssopus*), poached-egg flowers (*Limanthes*), and sage (*Salvia*), along with the aptly named bee balm (bergamot or Oswego tea plant, *Monarda*). Among the numerous flowers whose nectar has a magnetic effect on butterflies are candytuft

(*Iberis*), chrysanthemum, coneflower (*Echinacea*) and, of course, the butterfly bush (*Buddleia davidii*). A wildflower garden will also attract foragers and browsers, but in the interests of conservation, as mentioned above, it is recommended that you buy wildflower seeds, bulbs, or plants from a reputable nursery rather than lifting them from their natural environment.

Container Gardening

Another popular variation on the horticultural theme is container gardening, which offers a multitude of advantages. If you find it difficult to bend or move around with ease, for example, you can create a beautiful floral display in a container of the right size or height for you to tend. And if lack of space is a concern,

Left: *While poppies* (Papaver) *thrive best in situations where they receive full sun, lupines (*lupins, or Lupinus*) tolerate some shade and most soil types. Both make delightful additions to any wildflower garden.*

or you have no garden at all, you can still brighten the outside of your home with window boxes and hanging baskets. Judiciously planted and well-sited containers are also an invaluable way in which to hide an unattractive garden feature or to soften the lines of a patio, terrace, deck or pathway. A further benefit is their flexibility: they can be easily moved, dismantled, or rejuvenated. Containers are also ideal for growing herbs for culinary use, especially in the case of invasive herbs like mint (*Mentha*), which can otherwise run rampant through a flowerbed at breakneck speed.

As long as the container has a drainage hole, it matters little which type you choose: a terra-cotta pot (some of which are frost-proof), a wooden tub, a stone trough, an old ceramic sink, or any other vessel that catches your eye. However, there are a few basic principles that should be followed before planting. First, make sure that the container is clean and uncontaminated by any substance that may prove harmful to its living occupants; next, fill the base of the container with a layer of pebbles or crockery (perhaps the pieces of a broken terra-cotta pot) to aid drainage. Hanging baskets, which dry out quickly, should be given a water-retentive lining of moss or a punctured plastic sheet. Finally, fill the container about two-thirds full with a suitable potting medium and introduce your well-watered plants, carefully adding more soil with your

Below: As well as providing an arresting focal point, waist-high containers, like the handsome example pictured here, make ideal outlets for the creativity of horticultural enthusiasts who find kneeling or bending a struggle.

fingers until the container is nearly full to the brim and they are well bedded in. Water the container garden carefully, and remember that in the height of summer you will need to water at least once a day; your flowering plants will also thrive on prescribed doses of a suitable plant food.

The best time to plant up a container is in late spring, when the danger of frost is past; this applies particularly to annuals and tender perennials, many of which are perfect candidates for this form of gardening. *Impatiens* (informally known in Britain as busy Lizzies), begonias, pot marigolds (*Calendula*), fuchsias, lobelias, geraniums (*Pelargonium*), petunias, and pansies (*Viola* x *wittrockiana*) are only some of the rewarding plants that will provide a mass of vibrantly colored blooms all summer. Many varieties also have a trail-ing habit, making them ideal for hanging baskets and window boxes. A number of container-planting schemes are available to you: you could create interesting contrasts of color and texture by combining trailing perennials, like ivy (*Hedera*), or dwarf evergreens of architectural form, with brightly colored upright annuals. Alternatively, you could make an eye-catching feature of such spectacular bulbous plants as lilies (*Lilium*), or mass identically colored blooms within a single container. And if a particular plant comes to the end of its flowering season before its fellow occupants, you can easily remove it and replace it with a fresh specimen without disrupting the overall harmony of the display. What easier way could there be of creating a beautiful instant garden?

Above: Whatever type of garden you prefer, a wealth of stunning flowers of every habit and hue stands at your disposal for inclusion in your personal floral paradise.

Overleaf: Plant it in full sun, and the Hibiscus syriacus *will signal its gratitude with luscious blooms like these.*

Page 85: To ensure a striking summer display of dahlias, lift the tubers when frost threatens and store them in a dry, sheltered environment over the winter.

A Profusion of Color

The design of the charming garden above, at landscape artist Frederic Edwin Church's (1826–1900) Olana estate in the Hudson Valley, New York, appears to have been left to nature's whim, but its artless effect must have required much planning.

A Floating Paradise *Previous pages*

When siting water lilies (*Nymphaea*), their containers should be submerged beneath the surface of the water to a depth of between 9 inches (23 centimeters) and 1 foot (30 centimeters), depending on the species.

Beauty in Utility

The orderly scene on the opposite page is a view of the prolific herb garden at the self-sufficient community of Enfield Shaker Village, New Hampshire. The arrangement of these vigorous and colorful rows of plants is as beautiful as it is functional.

Contrasting Shapes *Overleaf*

Quite apart from their beautiful blooms, most long-stemmed species of lilies (*Lilium*) have attractive spiky foliage that provides an interesting contrast of height and form to neighboring plants.

Mexican Gold

The contours of the craggy landscape above, at Organ Pipe Cactus National Monument, Arizona, are echoed by the uncompromisingly architectural forms of the perennial cacti, while the vivid flashes of color provided by the multitude of Mexican Gold poppies (*Eschscholzia mexicana*) enliven the foreground of this dramatic vista. A poor soil is no deterrent to most poppies (*Papaver, Meconopsis,* and *Eschscholzia* genera), which unfold their petals in response to full sun.

Feathery Abundance   *Page 91*

The plumelike flowers of the *Celosia argentea* have earned it the common name of cockscomb. Plant it in a sheltered site in spring to ensure a spectacular summer display.

The Rewards of Opportunism

Neither the lupine nor the balsam root are fussy in their requirements when it comes to putting down roots, while their ability to seed prolifically ensures the continuation year upon year of wildflower meadows like the one pictured opposite, at Rowena Crest, Oregon.

A Poet's Paradise *Opposite*

To see a World in a Grain of Sand
And a Heaven in a Wild Flower,
Hold Infinity in the palm of your hand
And Eternity in an hour.

—William Blake (1757–1827)

An American Colonist *Above*

Although the white lupine (*Lupinus albus*) was cultivated in Europe from Roman times as animal fodder, it was not until the seventeenth century that Europeans began to appreciate the flower spikes solely for their beauty. The new fashion for the flowers occurred largely in response to the arrival of North American species, including the Virginian lupine (*L. perenne*), in 1637; the Californian tree lupine (*L. arboreus*), during the late eighteenth century; and the West Coast's perennial, or border, lupine (*L. polyphyllus*), in 1826.

What's in a Name?

Belonging as they do to the *Rhododendron* genus, some varieties of azalea (left) are often confused with rhodo-dendrons, and vice versa. Few people, however, need to know the plant's correct name to appreciate the breath-taking sight of its seemingly countless clusters of blooms.

Searching for the Sun

Many members of the genus *Convolvulus*, including the morning glory (below), will twine themselves tightly around a supportive structure in pursuit of their quest for the sun. In common with many flowering plants, dead-heading them regularly will encourage a longer period of prolific blooming.

Out of the Blue and into the Pink

The genus *Hydrangea* (below) includes climbers (*H. anomala* subsp. *petiolaris*) and bushy shrubs, but perhaps the best known are the extravagantly bloomed *H. macrophylla* mophead and lacecap varieties. Blue-flowering varieties will produce pink blooms if planted in alkaline soil, in effect acting as a litmus test if you are uncertain about the pH level of the earth in your garden.

A Profusion of Blooms

Lupines (*Lupinus*) stand rigidly to attention surrounded by a sea of phlox, above. After the wildflower was introduced to England from Texas in 1834, *Phlox drummondii* later returned to North America with an enhanced status as a prized garden flower. Indeed, all phlox varieties will reward the gardener with a multitude of vividly colored flowers in summer.

A Parade of Tulips *Overleaf*

See how the flowers, as at parade,
Under their colours stand displayed:
Each regiment in order grows,
That of the tulip, pink and rose.
—Andrew Marvell (1621–78)

A Genus of Many Varieties

The perennial and annual species that belong to the genus *Phlox* (above) number at least sixty. They include the popular perennial border phloxes, *P. paniculata* and *P. maculata*, the annual *P. drummondii*; the alpine *P. douglasii*; and *P. subulata*, the moss phlox, which the botanist John Bartram described to a colleague in 1745 as "the fine creeping lychnis."

Avid Climbers

Some clematis (opposite) are herbaceous flowering plants, but the majority are the perennially popular climbers, which send out petioles that entwine themselves around any nearby structure to anchor new growth, much as rock-climbers consolidate their positions before continuing their ascent. This is one of the most attractive early, large-flowering cultivars.

Spectacular Blooms and Dramatic Foliage

Although most rhododendrons (opposite) delight gardeners with a showy display of flowers in spring, since the majority are also evergreen, their glossy, lance-shaped leaves will provide a handsome foil for later-flowering plants—as long as these tolerate the acid soil that rhododendrons insist upon.

A Carpet of Floral Gems *Overleaf*

Typically smaller than the rhododendrons whose genus they share, and with more delicate blooms, evergreen azaleas are often commonly called Japanese azaleas. Unlike roses, azaleas do not require pruning, deadheading, or other routine maintenance, although to give of their best they do demand acid soil, a sheltered position in partial shade, and regular watering.

The Kindest Cut

To ensure that your rose bush produces blooms as large and prolific as those below year in, year out, it is vital that you prune it regularly (in spring or autumn) to remove exhausted stems and encourage vigorous new growth. Using a sloping cut, remove the stem just above an outward-facing, dormant bud.

Nature's Jewelry *Previous page*

There is something magical about the appearance of the fuchsia, a South American native whose decorative beauty has earned it the pleasingly fitting common name lady's ear drops. The genus *Fuchsia* today comprises a multitude of enchanting hybrids and cultivars boasting single, double, or semidouble blooms.

A Woodland Native

As its name suggests, the natural habitat of the low-growing wood sorrel (*Oxalis acetosella*, below) is the floor of deciduous woods. Interestingly, its leaflets fold up at night, as well as in cold and wet weather. Although the sight of wood sorrel growing wild is captivating, never dig up a plant to take home.

A Cautionary Tale

The sad fate of the lady's slipper orchid (opposite), the common name applied to the four genera of the *Cypripedieae* family (*Phragmipedium, Selenipedium, Paphiopedilum,* and *Cypripedium*) in Britain, serves as a cautionary tale to all would-be plunderers from the wild. Once a relatively common wildflower, the numbers of the *Cypripedium calceolus* have been so depleted by its removal from the wild that it is now in danger of extinction.

A Scent Evoked by the Sun

Gardeners value the honeysuckle (*Lonicera,* opposite) partly for its vigorous climbing habit, but perhaps mainly for the exquisite scent of its flowers, whose inimitable perfume hangs heavy in the air on balmy summer nights as an enticement to hawk moths. Some species, however, are notable for flowering during the winter months in warmer climates, including *L. fragrantissima, L. standishii,* and *L.* x *purpusii.*

A Magnetic Floral Personality

Commonly called the ginger lily or kahli ginger, *Hedychium gardnerianum* (above) provides a striking focal point in any garden, whether in a border or in a container. After all, whose eye could fail to be drawn by its spear-shaped leaves and spiky yellow flowerhead, which can measure up to 1 foot (30 centimeters) in length?

A Sea of Tiny Faces *Overleaf*

The first "faced" pansy (*Viola* x *wittrockiana*) is said to have been created by Mr. T. Thompson, a British aristocrat's gardener whose experiments in crossing *Viola tricolor* and *V. lutea* during the early nineteenth century resulted in what he described as "a miniature impression of a cat's face steadfastly staring up at me."

Success Guaranteed for Budding Gardeners

Marigolds (*Calendula officinalis*, opposite) are ideal flowers for impatient children to grow, because it takes only about ten weeks from the time when seeds are sown to the reward of glowing blooms, like this example, "Orange bon-bon."

Queen for a Day

The day lily (*Hemerocallis*, below) is so called because each of its flowers blooms for only a single day. They bloom prolifically, so that a daily succession of stunning flowers opens above the handsome, straplike leaves during the summer. Providing they have sufficient moisture, daylilies will thrive in most conditions.

Subtle Shades and Markings

The delicate flowers of the genus *Alstroemeria*, below, spring from perennial tubers and bloom profusely during the summer months. Their flaring petals, in shades of pink, orange, or yellow, are often streaked with contrasting colors. Erect stems and twisted, lance-shaped leaves make them a striking adornment to the garden, and the flowers are excellent for indoor arrangements because of their longevity and the beauty of their form and markings.

Oriental Allure

The tiger lily (*Lilium tigrinum*, opposite) first arrived in Europe from Guangdong, China, in 1804. Although it has an ancient pedigree as a culinary and medicinal plant in China and Japan, in the West it is prized for the exotic beauty of its orange, purple-spotted, "turk's-cap" blooms, a description that alludes to their turbanlike shape. The example shown is a wildflower in the Sun Peaks, near Kamloops, British Columbia.

A Festival of Fall Flowers

If you yearn for a showy display of blooms in late summer and fall, when many plants are reaching the end of their flowering season, consider planting a mophead hydrangea, or hortensia (*Hydrangea macrophylla*), shown at left. Remember to dead-head it in spring, to feed it regularly, and to water it well during the hot summer months, and it will respond in spectacular fashion.

The Apple of the Gardener's Eye

Few sights are so heart-ening in the spring as the exuberant display of deli-cate apple blossom, shown at right. Although *Malus* x *domestica* is the work-horse of the genus that provides us with apples for consumption, many other hybrids are culti-vated primarily for their crop of lovely blooms, among them *M. floribunda*, the Japanese crab apple.

A Perfect Specimen

Few flowers can compete with the sheer perfection of the water lily (*Nymphaea,* opposite). The flower's beauty is enhanced by the contrast of the round green leaves that surround it. No wonder that many Eastern cultures attribute divine qualities to this plant, which bursts into triumphant bloom above the mysterious waters of ponds and lakes.

An American Dream *Overleaf*

This stunning lavender-tinted landscape in Wyoming's Grand Tetons is carpeted with lupines (*Lupinus*), which flourish in great numbers during the brief summer season of the mountainous West.

Mexican "Daisies"

Zinnias (below) endow the garden with a riot of color in summer and endear themselves to the flower-arranger on account of their firm, elongated stems and long-lasting, colorful daisylike flowers. As befits natives of Mexico, they are vulnerable to frost, dislike the rain, and thrive best in full sun.

The Sun-loving Ice Plant *Page 124*

Although the genus *Mesembryanthemum*, to which the ice plant belongs, has been renamed *Dorotheanthus*, many gardeners still refer to it by its original name. These succulent, half-hardy annuals, which unfold their petals in response to the sun's rays, tolerate poor soil, including sand, which explains why the *Mesembryanthemum crystallinum* pictured here often flourishes in coastal sites.

The Glory of the Tropics *Page 125*

The grandly named *Bougainvillea glabra* "Magnifica" is commonly referred to as the paper flower on account of the delicate texture of its exotically hued floral bracts. Remaining true to its South American origins, this magnificent flowering vine, which can grow to heights of 30 feet (9 meters), demands a consistently warm, sunny environment to flourish, and will quickly decline if subjected to the frequently dull skies and frosty atmosphere of northern climes.

Garden Plant or Utensil?

Callistemon's common names, brush tree and bottlebrush, aptly describe the flowers (above) that bloom on the evergreen shrubs and trees of this genus—indeed, you could imagine cleaning the inside of a bottle with one, although the "bristles" are, in fact, stamens. If you try your hand at growing this attractive plant, make sure that it enjoys full sun and a neutral to acid soil.

Furry Fronds

Long, drooping scarlet catkins make this evergreen shrub, native to Malaysia (*Acalypha hispida*, opposite), a striking accent in the summer garden. Only the female plants bear these tassel-like flowers, which give rise to the plant's common names, chenille plant and red-hot cat's tail. This luxuriant bloom was photographed in Bermuda, an island that is renowned for its spectacular flowering shrubs and beautifully tended gardens.

A Floral Australian Arachnid

Gardeners are drawn to the unusual delight in flowering shrubs like *Grevillea* (opposite), with its evergreen, lance-shaped leaves and intriguing racemes of petalless blooms with protruding styles that inspired its common name, spider flower. A somewhat demanding native Australian genus, it requires an acidic soil, full Sun, and protection from frost, and is therefore often best grown under glass.

Red as Blood and White as Snow

The snow plant (*Sarcodes sanguinea*, above), a native of California, often pushes its way through a layer of snow carpeting the woodland floor of its preferred high-altitude habitat. Its species name, *sanguinea*, refers to its blood-red coloring.

A Prolific Self-propagator

One benefit of introducing a mallow (*Malva*, left) to your garden is the ease with which it self-seeds. These delightfully delicate, bowl-shaped blooms will multiply quickly if you let nature have its way.

A Communion With Nature

Solandra maxima's unusually shaped flowerheads (opposite) may suggest several analogies, but perhaps the plant's common name, chalice cup, fits it best, for the pendulous blooms do indeed resemble an inverted chalice or communion cup.

Blazing Lights of the Desert *Pages 132-3*

Although the common names of the ocotillo (*Fouquieria splendens*), which include candlewood, slimwood, coach whip, and flaming sword, are many and varied, each in its own way aptly describes either the tapering form of its spiny stems or the scarlet at their termini (although the color varies according to the species). Native to the American Southwest and Mexico, if the ocotillo is to feel at home in your garden, it will require desertlike conditions year round and will typically flower in response to the refreshing rains of spring.

A Plant with a Prehistoric Past

The fern- or palmlike members of the *Encephalartos* genus (above) that grow wild in tropical and subtropical regions are cycads, the direct descendants of plants that first gained a roothold in the earth around 225 million years ago. Although these scions of the *Zamiaceae* family bear striking blooms, their foliage is an equally attractive feature.

Birds of a Feather

The genus *Strelitzia* is commonly called bird of paradise (below) on account of the colorful, winglike flowers that suggest a flock of exotic birds alighing upon the evergreen stathes. *S. reginae* is also named the crane flower, no doubt because its stathes resemble cranes' beaks and its orange flowers, tufted, feathery crests.

A Pink and Pastel Pastorale *Overleaf*

Although the pea bush (*Lathyrus*) belongs to the *Leguminosae* (vegetable) family, it is cultivated for the beauty of its sprays of delicate, hooded flowers rather than for any culinary purpose. A hardy perennial, this plant appreciates well-drained soil and full sun and is a prolific self-seeder.

A Mixed Message

With a mass of prickly spines guarding each succulent stem (opposite), it's easy to see why the *Rebutia's* common name is the hedgehog cactus. The spines protect the plant from hungry predators, while the gorgeous blooms attract pollinators.

A Floral Fanfare

A native of Mexico and the American Southwest, the fleshy, prickle-studded stems of the organ-pipe cactus (*Pachycereus marginatus*, below), whose impressive height and upright growing habit inspired its common name, bear striking red and green-tinged white flowers.

Wildflower of the Golden West   *Page 157*

Like most members of the poppy family, *Papaveraceae*, the California poppy (*Eschscholzia*) thrives in the most unpromising of soils, springing up in luxuriant golden swathes across the grasslands of the Golden West, from its home state of California to Oregon.

A Southwestern Sunseeker

The agaves *(cây thừa)* of the *Agavaceae* family are divided into a number of genera, including the *Agave* and the *Lophophora*, although the *Leuchtenbergia* pictured above, which is often referred to as an agave, is a member of the *Cactaceae* family. The *Leuchtenbergia* grows in impressive numbers in the American Southwest, signaling its appreciation of the region's dry, sandy conditions and fierce sun with a proliferation of yellow flowers in summer.

A Focus of Attention

If you need a specimen plant to provide an eye-catching focal point for your garden, look no further than the yucca *(cây ngọc giá)* (opposite: the giant dagger yucca, photographed in Texas). With masses of white blooms borne on a stem that rises proudly above a spiky rosette of lance-shaped leaves, this summer-flowering plant defies you to ignore it. Plant it in a sunny position where it will have room to spread.

Flowers of the Desert

Delicate, colorful flowers bloom among the flat, spine-bearing joints of the aptly named prickly pear (*Opuntia*, opposite and below), enticing insects to pollinate them. Although the pear-shaped fruits are edible, most people would put them to a taste test only *in extremis*. Unless your garden offers hot, dry, desertlike conditions, prickly pears are best grown as houseplants.

Cut Flowers

An arrangement of cut flowers stimulates the senses, providing both a feast for the eyes and the heady fragrance that fills a room. Many of us have bought flowers on impulse, simply because they caught our eye in the florist's window and we were unable to resist their alluring beauty. Yet not only will the life span of many such flowers be short, since they usually have been imported from the countryside or even abroad, but they are also prohibitively expensive. Like any other business, floristry is also subject to the fads of fashion: starkly elegant, exotic blooms like the tiger lilies are "in" one year, only to be abandoned the next for a stylistic opposite; say the daisylike gerbera.

On the one hand, it is rather sad that nature's freely given bounty should have become a luxury item, but on the other, the booming florist's trade is an irrefutable proof of our passion for flowers. Unless you are lucky enough to have a greenhouse, you will probably always have to rely on your local florist to provide flowers that will not tolerate the climate of your area; otherwise, you can cultivate your favorite blooms economically in your own nursery—your garden.

Conditioning and Caring for Cut Flowers

Whether the flowers that you select to decorate your home are store-bought or garden-grown, there are a few simple procedures that should be followed before arranging them that will prolong their lives and hence the amount of pleasure they will give you.

Before arranging them in a container, you will need to condition, or prepare, your flowers. First, strip off any foliage that would stand below the waterline, because otherwise the water would cause it to rot, contaminating the vessel with bacteria and swiftly killing the blooms. In the case of roses, it is also best to remove the thorns, a prickly process that will be less hazardous if you wear gloves and perhaps also invest in a specially designed rose-stripper. With the stem laid bare, the next step is to cut the end at an angle, which will both refresh it and provide the maximum surface area through which the flower can take up water.

This is the basic conditioning treatment, but there are a number of other methods that will increase the longevity of certain flowers. The cut ends of woody stems, for example, like those of the lilac (*Syringa*),

Opposite: For many, the sunflower (Helianthus) epitomizes summer. Before arranging the blooms, condition sunflower stems by making a deep incision at the bottom, plunging them into hot water for a minute or so, and then transferring them to a container filled with cold water.

can be dipped in boiling water to seal them, thereby clearing any air blocks that would obstruct water uptake; searing the stems of flowers that are filled with sap, like the milkweed (or spurge, *Euphorbia*) and poppy (*Papaver*), performs a similar function. Such hollow-stemmed flowers as the lupine (*Lupinus*) will live longer if you turn them upside down, and then, using a watering can, fill the stem with water before plugging it with cotton. If your flowers have wilted (and it is best to cut them in the morning or evening), or have floppy stems, bunch the stems together and wrap a supportive collar of paper around them before standing them in cold water for a few hours; the stems will take up the water and will then become firm enough to handle without

being damaged. The boiling-water treatment is also an effective flower-reviver.

Finally, place your conditioned flowers in a suitable vessel filled with cold water. Some flower-arrangers also recommend adding a little sugar, a drop of bleach, or an aspirin to the water, but perhaps the most reliable option is to use a specially formulated cut-flower preservative, which generally contains energy-giving sugar and bacteria-killing ammonia. To keep your arrangement fresh, it is vital that you top up the water each day; during a spell of hot weather you may need to spray it gently with a reviving mist of fresh water. Remember, too, that any nearby fruit gives off ethylene gas, which will cause your flowers to mature earlier and therefore reach the end of their flowering period at a faster rate.

The Tools of the Flower-arranger's Trade

There was a time when flower-arranging was regarded as a discipline governed by a restrictive set of rules, any deviation from which was frowned upon. Today flower-arranging has been liberated into an exciting form of personal expression, in which floral artists are free to indulge their imaginations. Beauty is, after all, subjective, and a bunch of sapphire-blue cornflowers (or knapweed, *Centaurea*) arranged casually in a jar will delight the eye of one beholder as much as an ornately structured mantelpiece arrangement of grand hothouse blooms will satisfy another.

Before you unleash your creative powers and set to work, you will need a few pieces of equipment: either secateurs with which to cut tough stems, or a sharp pair of florist's scissors; a keen-edged knife or rose-stripper with which to condition

Below: Wicker baskets are an ideal foil for a display of flowers fresh from the garden. Because cut flowers need water, the basket should be lined or the flowers arranged in a watertight container.

stems; and a bucket filled with water in which to keep your flowers and foliage fresh, along with a watering can.

Although the only other essential item is obviously a vase or other type of vessel in which to arrange your flowers, a number of specialized aids (known as "mechanics") will give your creativity extra scope by allowing you a to anchor the individual components of your arrangement in place. The simplest—and prettiest—anchors are the translucent glass nuggets or marbles that are sold in an array of colors, or small pebbles that you could collect yourself; crumpled cellophane (plastic wrap) will also support flowers well. Water-absorbent floral foam (also known as plastic foam, or oasis), which you can buy in a variety of shapes and colors, is extremely useful, too: when soaked in water, this becomes soft enough to insert stems into at any angle, while at the same time holding them firmly in place. If the arrangement is very large, or the flowers substantial, you could package the floral foam in chicken wire (wire mesh or netting) to prevent it from crumbling under the combined weight of the blooms. Many flower-arrangers swear by the frog—a small disk supporting vertical prongs that are pushed into the floral foam to secure it. Others do without frogs and floral foam altogether, preferring instead a pinholder (or kenzan), a metal disk whose surface is covered with a grid of sharp pins into which stems are pushed. For even greater staying power, the base of the frog or pinholder can be attached to the bottom of the vessel with an adhesive clay (also known as stay soft, or oasis fix), plasticine, or florist's adhesive tape (oasis tape).

If you wish to create a natural-looking bouquet, you will find twine or raffia an invaluable way of holding the components

Left: The starlike formation of their red, cream, or pink bracts have made poinsettias (Euphorbia pulcherrima) symbolic of the Christmas season. Native to Central America, the poinsettia gives the longest-lasting display as a pot plant.

of your arrangement together. If you prefer a more sophisticated finishing touch to a rustic look, you could obscure the twine by binding a length of ribbon around it and then tying a bow as a final flourish (a glue gun will enable you to fix any stray or droopy elements of the ribbon in the desired position). Finally, among the host of other useful weapons in the florist's armory is thin florist's wire, which is used for binding, supporting, or extending plant material, and florist's tape (or stem-wrap tape), with which you can disguise florist's wire or seal the ends of stems.

Simple Guidelines for Flower Arrangements

Although you should let your inspiration be your guide, there are a few sensible flower-arranging tips that will help you to exploit your flowers' potential to the full. Plant material for flower-arranging is divided into three classifications: dominant, line, and filler material. As its name suggests, the dominant-material category comprises the most attention-demanding blooms that provide the main focus of the arrangement. Line material describes the components that give the arrangement structure and form, while filler material consists of foliage and smaller blooms with which you can fill any unsightly gaps or hide the arrangement's mechanics. Start by inserting the line material first, then arrange the dominant material, and finally, add the filler.

Your arrangement can be as complex or as simple as you like. Even a single perfect bloom will be a compelling magnet for the eye, whether you place it in a bud vase, or devise a more adventurous strategy for drawing attention to it. One unusual way of displaying a rose that has just passed the bud stage, for example, is to push its stem

Below: *Many types and styles of container are available to stimulate the flower-arranger's creativity: the brightly glazed Italian majolicaware pictured in this Venetian window scene, for example, is a perfect partner for vividly colored garden flowers.*

into a pinholder, place the pinholder in a glass vase and then fill the vase to the brim with water, thereby creating an instant floral aquarium. However, if you are itching to try your hand at a more intricate display, there are a few principles that you will find helpful regarding color, balance, proportion, scale, and style. Remember, too, to take the surroundings into consideration so that the room's furnishings and proportions do not detract from the arrangement and vice versa (a bowl of delicate nerines, for example, would be overwhelmed by a brightly patterned wallpaper.) Concentrating on the shape and hue of the flowers themselves will help to ensure successful, balanced, combinations.

The first thing that you generally notice about at a flower is its color (and in planning an arrangement you may find it useful to enlist the aid of a color wheel). One of four color options will probably suggest themselves: a monochromatic, single-colored, display; a polychromatic, or multicolored, arrangement; a combination of blooms of contrasting colors; or a medley of similarly colored flowers. Among the like-colored blooms, blues, violets, and white evoke a tranquil feeling, while reds, oranges, and yellows will create a more lively ambiance. The same principles apply within a polychromatic arrangement, with bright colors coming to the fore and cooler hues fading into the background, white blooms serving as highlighters.

The considerations of balance, scale, and proportion are interrelated and will to some extent be dictated by the shape of your plant material. If the end result is to appear harmonious, all of the floral elements should look balanced, or in proportion with one another and with the container—for instance, the large and dramatic blooms, like regal lilies (*Lilium regale*) would eclipse tiny ones, like lilies of the valley (*Convallaria majalis*). Certain flowers will inevitably act as focal points, whether on account of their color or their size, and if you want to achieve a balanced appearance, along with the illusion of movement, it is best to place these at the center, perhaps with a few at the bottom, too, before surrounding them with smaller blooms and foliage. In addition, make sure that the arrangement is literally well balanced, that is, stable—the last thing you want is for your lovingly collated work of floral art to collapse.

How you design with flowers is, of course, up to you, but you will usually find yourself creating either a facing (also called flat-back) arrangement, or an all-round display. Facing arrangements, which are intended to be viewed primarily from the front, are ideal for mantelpieces, while all-round displays, which will be seen from every angle, are the obvious choice for table centerpieces. Neither of these styles limits your imagination, however, for both offer you a multitude of options, including massing your flowers together, or creating a geometric, linear construction.

Vases, Bowls, Pitchers, and Unusual Containers

Another important component of arrangement style is the container, and you will need to consider the size, shape, color and material to which it is made when deciding on the vessel that will best complement the flowers. Provided that it is waterproof, you can use virtually any receptacle that inspires you, whether a proper vase or a less conventional type of flower-holder. Remember, however, that

it should be in scale with your blooms, as well as stable enough to support their weight. In addition, its appearance should echo the character of the dominant floral material: a willow basket or country-style pitcher will enhance the rustic appeal of cottage-garden flowers, for instance, while an austerely functional glass, porcelain, or aluminum vase will embellish, rather than detract from, the bold beauty of showy flowers like the belladonna lily (*Amaryllis belladonna*).

The more vases you can add to your collection the better, especially plain glass ones of different shapes and sizes, which offer a foolproof way of showing your blooms to their best advantage (make sure, however, that you keep the water crystal clear, as it, too, is on display—you could also add a few drops of food coloring for a really unusual effect). Other dedicated vessels include the bud vase and rose bowl, the first being designed to hold a single bloom and the second supporting a mass of blooms within its gridlike

Left: *The upright form of foxgloves* (Digitalis) *lends structure to arrangements. Because their stems ooze milky sap when cut, which contaminates the container and shortens their display life, the ends should be singed by passing them through a candle flame before arrangement.*

Above: A single tiger lily *(Lilium tigrinum) looks stunning displayed in a simple bud vase. Its pollen stains are hard to remove from fabric, so many arrangers remove the pollen-bearing anthers, which also prolongs the flower's vase life.*

metal cover. Bone china or earthenware vases, along with pitchers, can contribute greatly to both simple and glamorous arrangements (but if they are unglazed, and therefore not watertight, place a water-resistant base, like a saucer, under them to protect the surface on which they will stand). An urn-shaped vessel will give a Classical feeling to any arrangement.

A low, shallow receptacle lends itself extremely well to flowers that have weak or short stems. Many are sold specifically for Japanese-style arrangements, but you could also press a baking tin into service, filling a heart-shaped cake tin with a mass of red rose heads, for example, in a striking floral celebration for Valentine's Day. Indeed, many household utensils make surprisingly delightful containers, so take a look around your kitchen: you may be able to give a jelly mold, mug, cup, coffee or teapot—even a galvanized-metal or enamel pail—an entirely new lease on life.

Wicker baskets make ideal partners for robust, colorful flowers, as well as fragrant masses of delicate blooms like lavender. The best effect is achieved when they look jam-packed, so carefully cram in as many flowers as you can. If you think that

your displays would benefit from a brighter background, you can quickly disguise a wicker basket's natural color with a few bursts of spray paint; wooden trugs (or shallow gardeners' baskets) can be distressed with a thin layer of pastel-hued chalk (both are also easy ways of transforming terra-cotta pots). And a fascinating fusion of the high-tech and the traditional has resulted in baskets made of metal, which are now increasingly available. Clearly, however, no basket is waterproof, so before beginning your arrangement, you will need to line the basket with a sheet of polyethylene before inserting a block of floral foam, or else place a waterproof bowl inside it.

If the perfect container eludes you, you could always make your own. One idea is to clean a plastic bottle thoroughly and cut off the top section, resulting in a makeshift vase of the required height. Using a glue gun, stick a layer of leaves or twigs of the same height as the vase around the outside, then finish off by tying a raffia bow around your creation.

Creative Combinations

Since they are intrinsically lovely, it is rare that a display of garden flowers will be disappointing. One way of enhancing their beauty even more, however, is to juxtapose the blooms with lush green foliage, intriguing-looking seedheads, or even fruit (remember, though, that fruit emits ethylene gas as it ripens, thereby shortening both its life and that of any nearby plant material).

Ideally, foliage should echo the flower forms with which it is grouped so that it neither competes with them nor introduces a discordant note that disrupts the harmony of the arrangement. The feathery leaves of the asparagus fern (*Asparagus setaceus*) will provide a delicate foil for the angular spikiness of a colony of columbines (*Aquilegia vulgaris*), while the contoured, wheatlike leaves and flowers of the grass *Stipa gigantea* will bring another breath of the countryside to an arrangement of field or corn poppies (*Papaver rhoeas*). Another benefit of using foliage as a filler material is that it can provide a contrast of color and texture that will subtly emphasize the dominant floral material: subdued leaf colors or downy leaves, for example, encourage the eye to focus on the true stars of the arrangement, the blooms.

Among the many ornamental seed or flower heads (most of which can be dried) that will endow a flower arrangement with a captivating extra dimension are the blooms of the *Allium*, or onion, family and the exotic-looking Chinese lantern (or bladder cherry, *Physalis alkekengi*). Similarly, the teasels of the New Zealand burr (*Acaena*), globe thistle (*Echinops*), the sea holly (*Eryngium*), and rosehips, including the red seedheads of *Rosa rugosa scabrosa*, will bestow a feeling of warmth and fecundity upon any harvest arrangement.

When incorporated into wreaths for the table, door, or wall; garlands, or swags, the appropriate seedheads and foliage act as the embodiments of the season's spirit. (You could, of course, make your own wreath, garland or swag, but attractive ready-made versions are widely available.) Attaching a length of florist's wire to pine (*Pinus*) cones—either left *au naturel* or sprayed with gold or silver paint—and then inserting them into a wreath frame, along with some sprays of holly (*Ilex*), ivy (*Hedera*), and translucent mistletoe berries, will result in a tradi-

Left: *This field of sunflowers* (Helianthus) *blooming boldly among their leaves reminds us that most arrangements are enhanced by foliage. Leaves below the waterline should be stripped for optimum vase life.*

tional winter solstice arrangement that brings more than a touch of festive cheer to your home. In spring, you could combine yellow or white narcissi with furry hazel (*Corylus*) catkins. During the summer the oval green seed pods of the honesty flower (*Lunaria annua*)—which, as they dry, turn a translucent silvery-white—will make the perfect partners for a profusion of fragrant, pastel-colored sweet peas (*Lathyrus*) or violet salvias.

The posy is so named because in earlier, more romantic times, a gift of flowers was often accompanied by an eloquent poem (from the French, *poésie*) that spoke of the giver's love for the recipient. Despite the demise of this charming custom, flowers continue to speak for themselves. And through your flower selection and arrangements—from a simple tussie-mussie to an ornate bouquet, a grand floral statement, or a generous gesture of seasonal welcome—you, too, can give eloquent expression to the emotions and ideas that inspire you.

Golden Rules For Table Displays

Two exquisite flower arrangements (opposite) are focal points of this formally set dining table. They demonstrate two golden rules for such arrangements: they are not so high as to obstruct eye contact among the diners, and they are all-round displays, which are attractive when viewed from every angle.

Floral Cascades

The striking display below was created by massing tiers of potted poinsettia plants (*Euphorbia pulcherrima*). If you feel inspired to emulate its cascading effect, each element must be securely positioned, preferably in a dedicated potting rack, to avoid the possibility of an avalanche of tumbling plants.

Mophead Magic

The showy flowerheads of the mophead hydrangea (*Hydrangea macrophylla,* opposite) are supported by woody stems that need conditioning before arrangement to encourage the dispersal of air blocks. To do this, strip off a short length of bark around the bottom and plunge the stems first into boiling and then into cold water.

Detail in Design

Many elements enter into the creation of an arrangement as successful as the example below. The color combination should, of course, be harmonious and the dominant blooms—roses (*Rosa*) in this case—should be given center stage before you surround them with carefully placed filler material, which softens the overall effect and creates a sense of movement.

Color and Perspective *Overleaf*

The lighter and brighter a flower's color, the more it tends to stand out, while softer or darker hues seem to recede into the background. Thus experienced flower arrangers place deeper-hued flowers at the center and position those with lighter colors at the periphery to serve as highlighting accents.

Conditioning Roses *Page 157*

To prolong the beauty of cut roses (*Rosa*), many authorities advocate crushing the bottom inch (2.5 centimeters) of their tough stems with a hammer, which increases the surface area of the stem and enables better water uptake. Preservative powder, available from florists, and a cool environment also help keep roses fresh for a longer period.

A Bouquet of Summer Flowers

The vibrantly colored flowers of summer, like those shown on the opposite page, provide a wealth of creative possibilities for stunning indoor displays, ranging from container-based arrangements to wreaths, garlands, and swags.

A Floral Harvest

The freshly picked floral material laid loosely in the large wicker basket below demonstrates that basket arrangements should be densely packed with flowers and foliage unless the container itself is to become the focal point of the display.

Stars of the Garden

With their large, starlike blooms, lilies (*Lilium,* below) dominate any flower arrangement and are especially striking when massed together. Smaller and more delicate than the lilies, the other blooms used in this textural combination complement their stately beauty rather than competing for the viewer's attention.

Beauty in Simplicity

With their generous, daisylike blooms, coneflowers (*Echinacea*) draw the eye to the delightful arrangement above. The tall, wide-mouthed vase in which they stand is ideal for such long-stemmed flowers, because it supports the stems while encouraging the blooms to relax, giving the arrangement a deceptively artless appearance.

The Jewels of Spring *Previous pages*

After winter's muted colors, flower lovers eagerly await the season when tulips (*Tulipa*) burst into magnificent bloom. They are also easy to arrange, whether in a simple glass vase or as part of a more elaborate display. If your tulip stems are crooked, straighten them by bunching them together and wrapping them in newspaper up to the flower heads, standing the bundle in a tall, narrow container filled with water for several hours.

Creating Table Displays

Shallow containers like the ones above and opposite are ideal for table-center displays, which should be designed on a scale appropriate to the table and its settings. An integral feature of the rose bowl opposite is the supportive, gridlike lid into which the flower stems are inserted. Other types of shallow containers may need floral foam or pinholders to provide a stable medium to anchor the components in place.

In Praise of the Lily *Page 166*

I like not lady's slippers
Nor yet the sweet pea blossoms,
Nor yet the flaky roses,
Red or white as snow;
I like the chaliced lilies,
The heavy Eastern lilies,
The gorgeous tiger lilies,
That in our garden grow.
—Thomas Bailey Aldrich (1836–1907)

An Expression of *Joie de Vivre* *Page 167*

The robust, color-drenched dahlias, chrysanthemums, and *Rudbeckia* that comprise this summer display appear to be bursting with vitality. Multipetaled flowers like these are enhanced by massing them together.

A Marriage of Opposites

vật trang trí bàn ăn

The grandeur of the ornate Victorian epergne below has been softened by a charming arrangement of daisylike blooms. Although candleholders branch from the base of the vase, the creator of this attractive display has not used them, as candles would detract from the symmetry of the arrangement.

Elegant Artistry

Good placement of line material (above) makes for an imposing arrangement. However, when positioning long-stemmed blooms like gladioli (*Gladiolus*) at an angle, they must be anchored securely to ensure that they do not shift under their own weight.

Unusual Inspirations

To vary your arrangements, try using combinations of dried and artificial floral material, as well as herbs and fruits like the rosemary (*Rosmarinus*) and attractively shaped persimmon (*Diospyros*) that appear in the imaginative arrangement shown opposite.

Home-grown Exotica

The creator of the elaborate display below has enhanced the exotic appearance of its calla lilies (*Zantedeschia*) by using an oriental-style fan as a backdrop. Foliage and blooms of contrasting shapes and textures, including ivy (*Hedera*) and irises, also contribute interest and depth.

Summer-flowering Bulbs

The genus *Amaryllidaceae* comprises a rich variety of beautiful species, including the sea lily or sea daffodil (opposite). Pictured below is the delicate Peruvian daffodil, *Hymenocallis narcissiflora*. Many gardeners are reluctant to cut these fragile natural beauties for use in short-lived arrangements.

The Many-splendored Dahlia

A mass of multiformed dahlias in bloom suggests a brilliant bouquet for indoor use (opposite). When conditioning dahlias for arrangement, singe the cut ends of the stems to seal in the sap that would otherwise contaminate their vase water.

An Exuberant Display

Turk's-cap lily (*Lilium*) and bell-like fuchsia varieties (below) form a congenial partnership, the one opening its reflexed petals to the sun, the other bending toward the earth. However, the lilies will outlast the more ephemeral fuchsias in this arrangement.

A Celebration of Life

The arrangement opposite combines daffodils (*Narcissi*) in full bloom with their bulbs in an imaginative spring display that conveys the sense of burgeoning new life.

A Symphony of Line and Color

An unusual container like the one above enables the creative arranger to present even the most commonly displayed flora in a captivating new light. In this oblique arrangement, different varieties of *Narcissi* have been used with bare twigs to striking effect.

Flowers with a Message

The arrangement above, which features rosy-hued carnations (*Dianthus caryophyllus*), irises, and lilies (*Lilium*), would be a delightful gift on the birth of a baby girl. The freshly picked mass of colorful flowers and foliage shown at right includes the immortelles that signify eternal life.

Simplicity at Work

The loveliest arrangements are often the simplest, especially when the flowers are as beautiful as the roses (*Rosa*) seen here and on the following pages. Their unpretentious containers contribute to the artless effect of the full-blown flowers with their leaves and buds.

Fragrance and Flamboyance *Page 183*

Oriental hybrid lilies, like these beautifully mottled "Stargazers," feature large flowers that exude a heady, exotic perfume, borne on long stems. These lilies make a dramatic focal point and are relatively long-lasting in indoor arrangements.

Nature's Amen *Pages 184–85*

Fall is a poignant season for flower lovers: while nature delivers a consoling bouquet of late-flowering blooms like the sunflowers (*Helianthus*) and chrysanthemums in this handsome basket arrangement, they are the swan song of the floral year. In the words of Oliver Wendell Holmes (1809–94), "The Amen! of Nature is always a flower."

Winter Decor

The beautifully wreathed lavabo opposite and the brilliant arrangement below illustrate the colorful possibilities of such shrubs as the hardy firethorn (*Pyracantha*) and holly (*Ilex*), whose berries provide arrangers with a wealth of creative possibilities. Their use with poinsettias *(Euphorbia pulcherrima)*, or simply with dark green, glossy-leafed foliage, makes for richly colored, eye-catching seasonal displays.

The Lyrics of Spring *Overleaf*

In spring, when the first snowflakes (*Leucojum*) make their shy debut (page 188) to herald the later arrival of the Easter lily (*Lilium longiflorum*, page 189), we recall the joyous words of the Song of Solomon (2:10):

> *"For lo, the winter is past,*
> *the rain is over and gone;*
> *The flowers appear on the earth;*
> *the time of the singing of birds is come,*
> *and the voice of the turtle is heard in our land."*

A Miscellany of Materials *Previous pages*

Although their entrancing beauty and fragrance ensures that fresh flowers will almost invariably dominate a display, arrangements can be given additional depth, color, and interest through the careful placement of a variety of natural and artificial materials. Twigs, bulbs, acorns, and distinctively shaped leaves are just some of the fruits of nature's bounty that can be incorporated into a display. And why restrict yourself to the products of nature when letting your creativity run riot? Decorative paper, ribbons, twine, and silk flowers can all be used effectively to embellish your designs and containers.

Unconventional Partnerships

When you are planning an arrangement, take the quantity of flowers available to you, as well as their color, height, and shape, into consideration before settling on a suitable container. There is no reason why you should restrict yourself to a vase when your household probably offers many containers that might complement a display better. If masses of cut flowers await your attention, why not follow the example above and simply arrange them in an attractive bucket? Alternatively, teaming linear floral material with a stem-supporting, narrow-necked pitcher creates a winning partnership, as seen opposite.

Creative Uses for Flowers

It is ironic that although we often cannot resist picking flowers in order to admire their beauty at close quarters, in doing so we are hastening their deaths. With a bit of forward planning and a few basic techniques, however, it is possible to preserve their lovely appearance and delicate fragrance so that we can enjoy them for at least six months beyond their natural life span.

Herbalists and housekeepers have long practiced methods of harnessing the power of flowers to soothe ailments, provide valuable nutritional sources, and perfume both the house and body, while in Victorian times pressing and drying flower heads for decorative purposes became popular pursuits. This chapter outlines just some of the ways in which you can preserve and use flowers as a tonic for the senses, body, and soul.

Methods of Drying Flowers

There is almost no limit to the creative uses to which you can put dried flowers. Like fresh flowers, they can be arranged into beautiful floral displays, ranging from posies and pomanders, fireplace and mantelpiece features, to table decorations, swags, garlands, wreaths, and topiary trees. The principles for styling both fresh and preserved flowers are broadly similar, but remember that dried flowers are inevitably more brittle than their freshly cut counterparts and should be handled with care. To strengthen droopy or hollow stems, like those of the scilla, and to make them more flexible, you could bind them with thin florist's wire before drying them, gently inserting one end high up into the stem, and then, with the lightest of touches, spiraling the wire down the length of the stem.

There are a number of tried-and-tested techniques for drying flowers, some of which are better suited to certain floral types than others (space does not permit exploring all of them here, so you may wish to consult a specialist publication for details). All, however, encourage the gentle evaporation of moisture from the blooms so that the flower heads and stems are left intact and, notwithstanding some unavoidable changes in color, as attractive as when they were alive. In order to speed up the drying process, it is best to avoid harvesting blooms after it has rained—the optimum time is well into the morning on a sunny day.

Opposite: In times past, flowers were preserved to provide a year-round supply of materials used to perfume the house, alleviate ailments, and flavor food. Traditional methods of preparation and storage continue in this Massachusetts Shaker kitchen.

Above: *Casually bunched dried flowers make an eye-catching display inside or out, as seen on these handsomely embellished railings. However, direct sunlight will eventually fade the colors.*

Air-drying is the simplest method. You may bunch sprays of blooms like those of the sea lavender (also known as statice, *Limonium*)—preferably no more than ten, to allow the air to circulate more freely—and hang them upside down. Upright blooms like strawflowers (*Helichrysum bracteatum*) may be placed in a suitable receptacle, or laid flat during the drying process. (The flat-drying method is the best for fragile blooms and grasses, as well as for plant material for potpourris: you can either arrange them on a sheet of absorbent paper, like newspaper, or on a length of chicken wire or mesh, which will provide both support and maximum air flow.) In each instance, leave the blooms in an undisturbed spot, out of direct sunlight, where the air is warm and dry—an airing cupboard is ideal. Keep checking, and you will know the drying

process is complete when every part of the flower, including the stem, feels dry to the touch.

You could also enlist the aid of science to dry particularly prized or complex blooms, like panicles of lilac (*Syringa*), by using a desiccant, or glycerin, or putting them into your microwave oven. Silica gel, which is often sold by pharmacies, has overtaken more traditional desiccants, such as sand and borax, in popularity on account of its ease of use and efficiency. When preparing to use silica gel, first make sure that it is completely dry; if it appears to be retaining moisture, you can dry it by arranging the crystals on a baking sheet and placing it in a cool oven for twenty minutes. Next, cover the bottom of a flat plastic container with a generous layer of silica gel, arrange your flower heads on top, making sure that they do not touch each other, and then sprinkle them with more silica gel until every part of the blooms is covered, using a soft-bristled brush to work the gel into the nooks and crannies. Now place the container in a dark, warm place and monitor progress daily until the blooms feel dry, but not too dry, as there is a danger that they could crumble away into dust.

Glycerin, which is also available from pharmacies, is especially recommended for preserving fleshy foliage like that of the strawberry tree (*Arbutus*), and flowers that contain a lot of moisture, like camellias and magnolias, a process that may take weeks rather than days. Because the glycerin will be absorbed through the stem ends to replace the water within them, you will need to prepare the stems first by splitting them gently with a sharp knife and placing them in warm water for about two hours. Make up the glycerin solution by mixing one part glycerin with two parts hot water, pour it into a jar, and then stand the stems in the solution. Transfer the jar to a warm, dry spot and leave the glycerin to work until the plant material has changed color (you may have to top up the solution occasionally during the absorption period).

Microwaving your blooms has the great advantage of drying them speedily, but because drying times tend to be unpredictable (two minutes is a general guide), you will need to keep a hawklike eye on them and resign yourself to experimentation. Arrange your flowers between two sheets of kitchen paper, which will absorb the water that is drawn out of the flowers, set your microwave to half-power, and unleash the might of the microwaves.

Once your flowers have dried, if you are not intending to use them immediately, place them in a large paper bag or card container and store them in a dry place, as any humidity in the air will cause them to deteriorate. However you decide to arrange them—and you have a wealth of options—there are a few strategies that will help you to keep your display looking pristine. First, keep it out of direct sunlight to prevent premature fading; second, try to ensure that the surrounding air is not damp; and, third, blow away any dust with a hairdryer set on cool, slow mode.

Pressing Flowers

Most of us will have pressed a flower between the leaves of the book at some stage of our lives, usually to preserve a

***Below:** An excellent filler for dried-flower arrangements, sprigs of baby's breath (especially* Gypsophila paniculata) *are easily air-dried. Either stand them upright in a container, or bind their stems together and hang them upside-down until the drying process is complete.*

Above: *The sharp, distinctive taste of the fiery horseradish root* (Armoracia rusticana) *has long been used to add zest to sauces. Most kitchen gardeners grow this invasive plant in a pot, harvesting the root in fall, saving a section for replanting in spring.*

precious memory, or to try to capture the ephemeral loveliness of a wildflower that has caught our eye. Partly out of sentiment, and partly out of botanical fervor, the Victorians elevated this type of flower preservation to an elaborate art form—one that is still delightful today. And not only is pressing flowers child's play, it is also one of the best ways to preserve their vivid colors (remember, though, that the drying process will darken red-hued blooms).

When selecting flowers or foliage for pressing, make sure that they are both dry and relatively mature to ensure that the drying process is as short as possible. Because they contain a significant amount of water, it is unlikely that you will achieve as successful results with fleshy flowers

and foliage as with flatter, more papery, plant material. For this reason, too, it is best to cut bulky flower heads, like roses, in half with a keen-edged knife, and to separate florets and clusters of flowers. In addition, calyxes should be removed by cutting as close to the flower head as possible, and if you decide to retain a succulent stem, squeeze it gently between two sheets of kitchen paper so that it releases as much moisture as possible.

Whether you prefer the convenience of a commercially made flower press, or the various cheaper, perhaps more versatile, homemade alternatives, is a matter of personal choice, although the latter will give your creativity more scope. They include folding a sheet of blotting paper around your flowers, inserting it into a hardback book (but not one that you really value, in case the juices stain the pages), and placing the book in a warm, dry spot with a heavy object weighing it down. In the case of substantial plant material, you could sandwich it between sheets of brown paper and stow it under your mattress. Both methods require a drying time of at least six weeks. If you can't wait this long, and your plant material is relatively thin, you could always encase it in blotting paper and run a moderate iron over it—if you don't mind the smell.

Few greetings cards will be more treasured than one you have made yourself. And even if you are dubious about your artistic skills, nothing could be simpler than assembling a selection of pressed flowers and foliage to form a miniature garden. All you need is a folded piece of good-quality card stock, a sharp pair of scissors, some PVA (white) glue, and transparent adhesive paper with which to seal in your floral design. Other fresh suggestions include securing your dried flowers between two pieces of glass to make a picture, trapping them within clear casting resin poured into a mold to make an eye-catching paperweight, and sticking them to a photograph frame or lampshade before coating them in a protective layer of nonflammable varnish. Once you are alive to the many decorative uses for pressed flowers, the creative possibilities are virtually endless.

Olfactory Delights

It is hard to imagine, but in the long-gone days when people bathed infrequently and such labor-saving devices as washing machines and vacuum cleaners, not to mention the local dry cleaner, had not yet been invented, the average house must have smelled distressingly rank. Without the battery of cleaning products available to today's homemaker, the mistress of the sixteenth-century household did what she could to perfume her home, drying sweet-smelling flowers, like rose petals, mock-orange blossoms (*Philadelphus*), honeysuckle blooms (*Lonicera*), and the carnations and pinks of the *Dianthus* family, as well as herbs, to place in bowls, strew over the floor, and scent the household linen. We have retained the customs of scenting our clothes with sachets of dried lavender (*Lavendula*) and of placing potpourris around the house, and, indeed, both are easy to make yourself, rather than buying commercial products. You will find that experimenting with dried potpourri ingredients is an absorbing

Left: *As its name suggests, heartsease (or pansy,* Viola tricolor*) has traditionally been used as a remedy for the sadness caused by a "heavy" or "broken" heart. Modern herbalists also use it to treat a variety of complaints including high blood pressure (hypertension), palpitations, some skin disorders, and pulmonary conditions.*

Right: *Fruits and vegetables can be combined creatively with blooms to add an interesting dimension to a floral display. Featuring dried daffodils (*Narcissus *cultivars), peppers, citrus fruits, and bulbs, this arrangement's theme is the fruits of the earth.*

process, conjuring up a variety of evocative fragrances that may recall a particular season or an exotic or rural location, especially if you choose a container—be it a country-style basket or a delicate china bowl—that underlines the association.

In times past, dried flower heads and petals were combined with fragrant herbs like lavender, mint (*Mentha*), rosemary (*Rosmarinus*), and thyme (*Thymus*), and with rich-smelling spices: cinnamon and allspice, tangy roots, dried citrus peel, and aromatic selections of wood and bark. Fixatives included powdered orris root (which is made from the rhizomes of *Iris florentina*), and floral oils. The essential ingredients have hardly changed to this day, although we now generally enhance a potpourri's appearance by including dried seed pods, foliage, and other types of plant material for visual interest.

When making a potpourri, you have a choice between the dry (the simplest and most visually appealing) and the moist (the more traditional and richer-smelling) methods. In the first, the potpourri ingredients are air-dried either by the hanging or flat-drying technique (the latter is advocated for rose petals), after which they are combined, transferred to a covered plastic container, and stored in a warm, dry place to allow the fragrance to develop. After about six weeks, mix in a small amount of a natural fixative, like dried orris root, gently with a wooden spoon and assess the fragrance—at this stage you could intensify it by adding a few drops of floral oil. Transfer the mixture to a paper bag, roll down the top, and give it a thorough shake before storing it in a dark place for at least six weeks, shaking it every day during the first week and once a week thereafter.

The moist method involves curing the floral ingredients with salt—and often brown sugar or brandy also—and storing them in a preserving jar for a longer period (the smell improves with time) before adding in the fixatives and oil. Although they smell stunning, potpourris made according to this method do not look very alluring, so they are usually transferred to specialized containers with perforated lids or earthenware pomanders. Alternatively, you could fill a number of small muslin bags with the moist mix, much as you would make a lavender sachet, and then hide them within a dry-mix potpourri, place them in a linen closet or drawer, or in a pillow to induce sleep, or infuse them in your bathwater.

The floral oils that enhance the intensity of a potpourri's aroma have many other therapeutic uses, too. The ancient Egyptians, Greeks, and Romans all perfumed their bodies with oils made from flowers and herbs, but it was the Arab physician Avicenna (AD 980–1037) who perfected the art of distillation, that is, extracting a flower's essential oils, the most widely used being the damask rose (*Rosa damascena*), resulting in "attar of roses." The essential oils that are used in aromatherapy are industrially produced by means of a steam-distillation process and, because they are both powerful and volatile, should be used with care. You can, however, make your own rose oil (or any other floral or herbal oil) by pouring a bottle of vegetable oil into a bowl and cramming it with as many petals as you can fit in; then let the mixture infuse for two days. Next, transfer the mixture into a sieve, and, using a wooden spoon, press down hard so that the perfumed oil drips into a bowl placed beneath it. Finally, pour the rose oil into a container that has an airtight lid and use it for adding to potpourris or as a scented massage or bath oil.

Titillating the Tastebuds

Until the eighteenth century, when it acquired its modern meaning, "potpourri" (the French for "rotten pot") described the mixture of vegetables and meats contained within a kitchen stockpot. And although we still use a range of herbs and the preserved buds of the caper flower in cooking, as well as candied flowers in baking, we may be unaware of the important role that flowers played in flavoring the cuisine of the past, or of the myriad uses to which they can still be put.

However, there are a few vital *caveats* that you should remember before using flowers in the kitchen. First, you must be certain that they are edible: if you are

Below: The yarrow's botanical name, Achillea, recalls its mythological use by the Greek hero Achilles for healing wounds sustained in battle. Yarrow contains tannins that inhibit bleeding, resins that are antiseptic, volatile oils with anti-inflammatory properties, and silica, which promotes the growth of new tissue.

Right: *The leaves of many varieties of mint (*Mentha*) are used to refresh the palate, aid digestion, and soothe digestive disorders, while the taste of spearmint (*Mentha spicata*) has inspired the manufacturers of chewing gum and toothpaste, and that of peppermint (*Mentha piperata*), the makers of confectionery.*

unsure, consult an authoritative source (the names of a few reliable books are given in the bibliography). Second, do not use flowers that you know, or even suspect, have been treated with pesticides, including those sold by florists, and wash and dry your blooms thoroughly before use. Finally, do not serve edible flowers to children, allergy sufferers, or people who may have a compromised immune system, as they could induce adverse reactions.

There are a number of herbs and flowers that make delicious teas, including laven-der (purportedly Queen Elizabeth I of England's favorite refreshment), mint, chamomile (*Chamaemelum*), rosehips, lemon verbena (*Aloysia triphylla*), and various vitamin C-packed varieties of gera-nium, including the peppermint-flavored *Pelargonium tomentosum* or *P. graveolens,* and the lemony *Pelargonium crispum* varieties. A basic recipe is to place 2oz (50g) of fresh, or 1oz (25g) of dried, blooms or leaves in a teapot; pour 1 pint (600ml) of boiling water over them; leave the tea to infuse for ten minutes; and then strain it.

You can either drink the tea at once, while it is still warm, perhaps sweetened with honey or sugar, or chill it in the refrigerator (it will usually keep for up to two days). Herbal or floral butters are also easily prepared with such natural flavor-enhancers as society garlic (*Tulbaghia violacea*) by combining them with softened, unsalted butter; chilling the mixture and shaping it into log form; and pressing some reserved flowers around the outside as a final decorative touch. Another idea is to scent sugar with rose petals, vanilla pods, or the fragrant leaves of such geraniums as *Pelargonium grossularioides* (whose aroma is reminiscent of coconuts), *P. capitatum* (roses), and *P. odoratissimum* (apples), by alternating layers of sugar and petals or leaves in an airtight storage jar.

There are many enchanting decorative ways with flowers, too. One is encasing small, single blooms (violets, *Viola odorata*, are ideal) in ice cubes by filling an ice-cube tray half full of water and freezing it for about four hours, placing a bloom in each compartment, carefully covering each with water, and then freezing the floral ice cubes until needed. Another variation on the iced-flower theme is to fill a large transparent bowl partway with water and small flowers; set a smaller bowl within it, displacing the water to the top of the gap between the two bowls; and put the double bowl in the freezer until the water has turned to ice. Alternatively, hibiscus flowers (*Hibiscus rosa-sinensis*), as well as tulips (*Tulipa* cultivars), are guaranteed to create a talking point when used as receptacles for individual portions of dessert (but remember to remove their stems, pistils, and stamens first). And what simpler way to enliven a salad than by sprinkling it with cucumber-flavored borage blooms (*Borago*

officinalis), or garnishing a dish with dill flowers (*Anethum graveolens*), nasturtiums (*Tropaeolum majus*), or even fuchsias?

If the thought of incorporating flowers into your culinary repertoire intrigues you, consult a dedicated edible-flower guide for more ideas on cooking safely with a veritable A to Z of blooms, from those of the arugula (*Eruca vesicaria*) to the zucchini (*Cucurbita pepo*). Whether you add them to salads, soups, or stews, you are certain to be showered with compliments, as well as inundated with requests for your "secret" recipe.

Below: *Both the common and botanical names of "English" lavender (*Lavandula officinalis*) are derived from the Latin verb lavare, "to wash," reflecting the Roman practice of sprinkling these fragrant flowers into bathwater. Lavender tea was said to be highly favored by Queen Elizabeth I of England.*

Witches' Bane

In more superstitious times the starbursts of mauve flowers produced by chives (*Allium schoenoprasum*, opposite) were hung on the door to repel witches. The flowers remain popular for ornamental use in dried flower arrangements and potpourris, while the chopped leaves are often used to flavor vegetable dishes, and the edible flowers make a colorful garnish.

Salvation

Although wild sage is considered too pungent for culinary use, the leaves of many cultivated sages, including the scarlet-bloomed sage (*Salvia rubiflora*) pictured above, are prized by cooks for their flavor. The Latin name is derived from the verb *salvare*, to save or heal, and in addition to using it to foster health and well-being, the Romans considered the plant sacred.

The Indoor Country Garden

Whether fresh, in the process of drying, or fully dried, garden flowers and herbs endow the home with a charming, rustic atmosphere. The scene above at the Hancock Shaker Village, Massachusetts, includes an inverted bouquet of air-drying flowers and some of the community's traditional garden tools. A rich variety of flowers appears to be roosting in the rafters of the old house opposite. The attic is one of the best places to air-dry flowers by the hanging method, particularly if it is warm and dry. Many experts advocate that a windowless environment helps the flowers retain optimum color.

A Cornucopia of Autumn Color *Previous pages*

The fruits of fall, including pumpkins, squashes, sunflower seedheads, and corn cobs, offer a multitude of creative possibilities for an eye-catching harvest or Thanksgiving display. Corn cobs (*Zea mays*) should be air-dried in an upright position, while sunflower (*Helianthus*) seedheads should be placed on absorbent paper and supported on a mesh or wire rack during the drying process, which in both cases may take a few months.

Benign Protection

Scarecrows were originally fashioned to deter birds from food crops, although many now serve simply as decorative folk art, as shown at right. Lavender (*Lavendula*) is also credited with powers of repulsion: once sacred to Hekate (Hecate), the Greco-Roman goddess of witchcraft, it was believed to deflect the malignant gaze of the evil eye. Its volatile oils repel insects including moths, flies, and mosquitoes, hence the traditional use of sachets of dried lavender flowers in drawers and closets to protect clothing from moths.

Natural Artifice

Floral creativity need not be limited to arranging cut or dried blooms and foliage for the house. What setting could be more appropriate for the artfully designed display shown below of flowers, foliage, and bird's nest than its natural habitat, the garden?

The Remains of the Daylily

The exquisite blooms of the daylily (*Hemerocallis*, opposite) may last only for a day, but because they are edible (the taste varies according to the species), enjoyment of the flowers can be extended by incorporating the buds, petals, and leaves into soups, salads, and stir-fries.

A Potent Healer

The roots of some species of coneflower (*Echinacea*, opposite) have been used for many centuries throughout several Native American culture areas for their antiseptic, anti-inflammatory, and anesthetic qualities, but the coneflower's healthful properties have only recently become more widely recognized. As a herbal remedy, the most popular use of the easily cultivated perennial purple coneflower (*Echinacea augustiflora*) today is to boost the immune system.

Nostalgic Fragrance and Form

"... roses, damask and mossed,
Scenting the English air with France and Persia,
Sulphur and shell pink, they keep close company
With dew pearls, ladybirds."
— From *Old-fashioned Flowers*, Leonard Clark.

From Garden to Table

The ephemeral flowers of the daylily (*Hemerocallis*, above) are as delightful at the table as in their profuse, multi-colored splendor in the garden. A native of Peru, the nasturtium (*Tropaeolum majus*, opposite) has been used in Western cuisine since its introduction to Europe by the Spanish conquistadors. It is also known as Indian cress for the peppery taste of the flowers, buds, seeds, and leaves, which are often used in salads.

Fragrant Potpourris

Potpourris (above) can be made using either the dry or moist method. The former results in highly decorative mixes ideal for display in shallow dishes and other open containers. The advantage of the moist method, in which the petals are preserved in an alcohol and sugar mix, is that it intensifies the perfume of the floral ingredients, but because such mixes can be unattractive, they are usually placed in closed containers with perforated lids.

Wreathed in Flowers

A traditional sign of welcome is the evergreen or dried-flower wreath on the door, as seen in the photograph below. The passage of the year can be marked by tucking the flowers and foliage of each season in and around the circular form that is a symbol of eternity and the cyclic renewal of the natural world.

Woodland Bounty

Nature showers the home decorator with the ready-dried fruits of trees like the fir (*Abies*), larch (*Larix*), and pine (*Pinus*). Because their forms resemble those of Christmas trees, cones are especially effective in winter-themed swags, garlands, and wreaths. They can be left *au naturel*, as above, or sprayed with gold or silver paint to lend a more festive appearance.

Scents and Sensibility

The appearance of a potpourri mix owes much to its container, as seen in the examples opposite. Perforated china pomanders are suitable for a moist mix, which suffuses a room with a heady fragrance, while the visual appeal of a dry mix gives the imagination more scope. Vases, bowls, cups, and decorative tins are among the many household objects that can be pressed into potpourri service.

Floral Ornamentation

Flowers have been a fertile source of inspiration to artists and craftsmen over the millennia, initially for the symbolic expression of sacred concepts, and in more recent times for their purely decorative beauty. And when artists began to treat flowers as a primary, rather than subsidiary, subject—a trend that reached its peak during the seventeenth century with the marvelously detailed still lifes of the Dutch and Flemish masters—it was inevitable that flower depiction would make another leap, from the rarefied realm of fine art to the more generally accessible province of home furnishings.

In ancient Egyptian pharaonic art, depictions of the lotus, or waterlily, representing Upper Egypt, can often be seen intertwined with those of the papyrus plant, the symbol of Lower Egypt, the *sema tewy* emblem formed thereby signifying the "union of the two lands." In such funerary texts as the Book of the Dead, many other flowering plants feature prominently, too, including cornflowers and poppies, reflecting their usage in everyday life for ritual and personal decoration. The sophisticated belief system of the ancient Egyptians is now extinct, but many ancient religions that are still practiced today accord a similarly important symbolic status to the lotus, whose primary significance in ancient Egyptian art was rebirth. The sacred art

Opposite and below:
Elaborate floral headdresses remain an integral part of the costumes worn by performers of Indonesia's traditional dances.

223

Above: A variety of flowers, including the lotus, an important symbol of rebirth, are prominently featured among the offerings made to the gods in this scene from the Egyptian Book of the Dead.

of Buddhism, whether in its Chinese, Japanese, or Indian forms, has changed remarkably little since its inception, and modern representations of both Buddha and the bodhisattvas (broadly equivalent to Christianity's saints) still incorporate stylized lotuses, the primary emblem of the Round of Existence. Although Islamic art prohibits the representation of living things, a floral influence is discernible in the rosette shapes seen in wall hangings, carpets, and tiles: they form a fundamental part of the otherwise geometrically dominated style of Muslim art. It is from Islamic artwork, too, that the stylized flower-and-foliage "arabesque" and "moresque" patterns woven into the fabric of damask (which was first produced in Damascus, Syria, during the fourth century) are derived.

As seen earlier, traditional Christian art contains a wealth of floral symbolism, and even when the Roman Catholic painters of the Renaissance began to broaden their repertoire by embracing "pagan" Classical themes, their inclusion of certain types of flower conveyed a specific, coded message that was widely understood. A direct link with the floral symbolism of Classical times lives on in many homes today in the form of the ceiling rose, whose story also explains the meaning of the Latin phrase *sub rosa* ("under the rose"). According to Greco-Roman myth, Eros (Cupid) once presented Harpocrates with a rose, the emblem of Aphrodite (Venus), in an attempt to persuade the god of silence not to reveal the goddess of love's amorous indiscretions. Thus the rose became a token of secrecy and evolved into the ceiling rose, which reminded people who attended secret gatherings not to disclose details of their deliberations to outsiders. Similarly, Roman Catholic confessionals are often decorated with roses as a sign that the sanctity of the confessional must not be betrayed by the priest.

In the days before the invention of central heating and wallpaper, those who were rich enough often insulated their homes with tapestry hangings portraying edifying Christian scenes and allegories. For example, a beautiful series of six French tapestries collectively titled *La Dame à la Licorne* (The Lady and the Unicorn) was made during the late fifteenth century for Jean Le Viste of Lyon. Although the overall theme is chivalric, five of the tapestries are concerned with the senses of smell, touch, taste, hearing, and sight. All are strewn with a multitude of flowers, and, indeed, it is from France that the decorative style featuring a repeating motif of tiny blooms, known as millefleurs ("a thousand flowers"), is derived. The tapestry illustrating the sense of smell is especially evocative of the fragrance of flowers: *La Dame* is depicted twining blooms offered by her maidservant into a floral circlet, while a monkey (symbolizing humankind) sniffs at a particularly beautiful flower.

Such Gothic and heraldic styles, which were typical of the Middle Ages and also featured in woven and embroidered bedcovers, persisted into the sixteenth and seventeenth centuries. They were superseded during the eighteenth century by Palladian Classicism and the exuberant rococo style, in which flowers figured prominently. Now the influence of India and China began to be felt, too, with imported, flower-bedecked porcelain,

silks, and wallcoverings lending an exotic touch to many wealthy European homes and encouraging a host of cheaper chinoiserie imitations. The stylistic barometer then swung toward the architectural motifs of Neoclassicism, that is, until the mid-nineteenth century, when Victorians began to embrace an eclectic cornucopia of period styles and foreign influences. It was not until the Victorian era, with the

Below: *This detail from an exquisite Turkish miniature depicts Eve in the flower-strewn Garden of Eden before the fall of humankind. In Jewish, Christian, and Islamic belief, paradise is suffused with the divine fragrance of blooms.*

Above: *Floral motifs have adorned prized pieces of Western china since the eighteenth century, when leading European manufacturers like Sèvres, in France (established in 1756), and Meissen, in Germany (1710), perfected the hitherto Chinese art of making fine porcelain.*

pared-down forms of *Japonisme* and the Japanese predilection for elegant blooms like the magnolia, chrysanthemum, and jasmine; Arts and Crafts drew its inspiration from the indigenous flowers commonly depicted in Europe during the Middle Ages. Indeed, both movements gave flowers an elevated place in their stylistic vocabulary. Notable British aesthetes like Walter Crane (the illustrator of *Flora's Feast*, a celebration of flowers published in 1889); designer Christopher Dresser (a botanist); and E. W. Godwin all incorporated sunflowers, lotuses, and pinks (carnations and similar plants of the genus *Dianthus*) into their works. Emulating his medieval predecessors, William Morris, the leading light of the Arts and Crafts movement and a keen gardener, preferred instead to celebrate a host of such humble meadow and hedgerow blooms as columbines, larkspurs, and honeysuckle in his naturalistic wallpapers and textiles. Rare was the cast-iron Victorian fireplace that was not framed by two vertical rows of slip tiles decorated with floral designs, whether they were transfer-printed with realistic blooms; the Islamic-style fantasies of the Arts and Craftsman William de Morgan and his colleagues; or any of the other host of styles that prevailed during this period of fevered creativity.

Hot on the heels of these influential movements came Art Nouveau, the "new art" that flourished during the 1890s until its decline around the time of World War I. This gloried in sinuous, stylized floral forms, so much so that it was sometimes called *Stile Floreal* (Floral Style) in Italy. Waterlilies, Asiatic lilies, poppies, and wisteria were especially popular, partly because to the Belle Époque eye they rep-

Industrial Revolution in full swing, that working people were able to afford inexpensive, machine-made home furnishings. Mass-produced wallpapers, fabrics, rugs, furniture, and other household items began to flood the marketplace. And many of them were densely decorated with popular flowers, especially full-blown roses, rhododendrons, pelargoniums, and hydrangeas, as well as the more delicate lilies, orchids, and fuchsias.

The most important decorative styles of the late nineteenth century were those of the Aesthetic and Arts and Crafts movements. Aestheticism espoused the

resented the height of sophistication, and partly because they provided stunning subject matter. Indeed, in the meltingly organic forms created by the French master of glass Emile Gallé, or in the luminous stained-glass windows and lamps of the American designer Louis Comfort Tiffany, such floral forms took on a color and vibrancy that has rarely been equaled. Furthermore, the posters of one of the period's most popular—and emulated—graphic artists, Alphonse Mucha, often featured voluptuous young women whose curves were echoed and underlined by the floral forms that entwined them. Flowers in a very different style also informed the work of the influential members of the Glasgow School of Art in Scotland, notably architect and interior designer Charles Rennie Mackintosh. He favored the tulip and the pale-pink rose that formed the basis of the abstract "Glasgow rose" motif.

With the emergence of Art Deco in 1925, and subsequently Modernism, the popularity of floral interiors waned, with more austere, abstract, and functional designs predominating. During the 1960s, however, the floral motifs of Art Nouveau regained favor, while during the style-conscious 1980s there was renewed interest in the florid floral chintzes popularized by Sybil Colefax and John Fowler. The Arts and Crafts style enjoyed a similar revival. At the same time, flowers gained a new champion in the Welsh-born fabric designer Laura Ashley. Today's diversity of taste, and a more relaxed attitude toward interior decoration, are reflected by the fact that floral motifs are neither "in" nor "out." Many manufacturers offer a permanent stock of flower-based fabrics, wallpapers, and wallpaper borders.

Floral Interior Decoration

As we have seen, there are many ways in which you can bring the beauty of flowers into your home, from an arrangement of fresh garden flowers, to a fragrant floral potpourri or a colorful furnishing fabric. You could also follow tradition by decorating your walls and furniture with stylized blooms yourself. Indeed, flowers are among the most popular folk-art motifs: their stylized forms were stitched

Below: Whether applied to architecture, furniture, or objets d'art, stylized flower forms were the favored decorative motifs of the late nineteenth century for both the eclectic Victorian style and Art Nouveau.

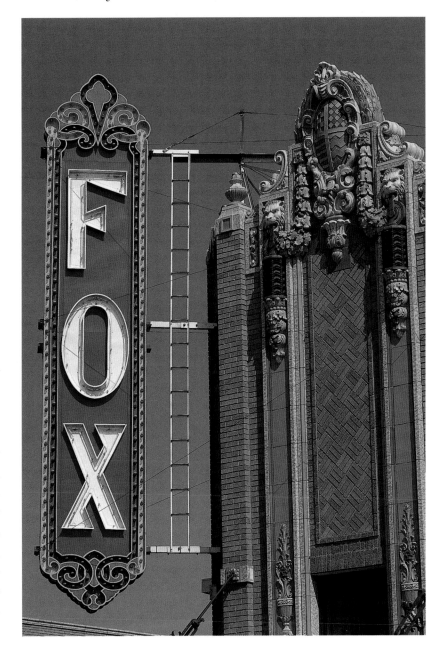

Above: *Morris, Marshall, Faulkner & Co., the firm founded by William Morris (1834–96) in 1875, became famous for the naturalistic floral-and-foliate patterns that appeared in textiles, carpets, and wallpapers like this one.*

into the household linen or painted onto homely furniture during long winter evenings. The tulip, with its connotations of the Holy Trinity, was especially loved by traditional Christian households, as were floral garlands and rosettes. If you enjoy needlework, or are an enthusiastic artist, you could follow in these footsteps, but if you are less confident of your artis-

tic skills, two of the easiest crafts to try are stenciling and découpage. (Only the rudiments of these techniques are outlined here, so if you are interested in learning more about them, many specialist publications are available.)

Découpage (from the French *couper*, "to cut," and *de*, "out of") has its origins in the seventeenth century, by which time engraving and printing techniques had become relatively sophisticated, and Europeans were delighting in the newly imported treasures from the Far East, including intricately decorated, lacquered, or "japanned," furniture and household objects. Because the originals were far beyond the financial reach of most people, a cheaper alternative was developed in Italy—*arte povera* (or "impoverished art")—whereby the subjects of printed engravings were cut out, affixed to furniture, and then coated with protective lacquer. The technique spread rapidly throughout Europe, taken up enthusiastically by manufacturer and also by the "idle rich," who could afford both the prohibitively expensive prints and the valuable time involved. By the nineteenth century, the new lithographic printing process had made good-quality prints widely affordable, and a craze developed for covering any available surface, be it a wall, desk, vase, or tray, with cutout prints and even postage stamps.

You can do the same by selecting any attractive floral print (but preferably one printed on good-quality, medium-weight paper in nontransferable ink) from a book or calendar, for example, and either cutting it out with a sharp pair of scissors, or, if you do not wish to cause irreversible damage, having it photocopied in conformity with the laws of copyright. You could also use offcuts of dress or furnishing fabrics. Make sure that the surface of the object to which you intend to apply your design is smooth and clean, then cover the back of the cutout with white glue or matte medium and stick it in place. Next, smooth down the design carefully and wipe off any excess glue. When the glue has dried, use a soft brush to apply as many coats of a clear or tinted finishing product, like acrylic varnish, as you feel are needed, allowing each coat to dry thoroughly before applying the next.

Photocopied prints also provide good basic designs for stenciling, a technique that evolved through the ingenuity of people who wished to enliven their plain walls, but couldn't afford costly wallpapers. Using a piece of tracing paper and a soft pencil, trace over an original or photocopied design and then transfer the tracing to a piece of stiff cardstock. Cut out the design with a sharp pair of scissors, and you now have your stencil. Make sure that the wall or object to which you intend to apply it is clean and smooth, and that any paint you may have applied as a background color is completely dry. Then hold, or temporarily attach, the stencil to it and draw round its outline with an erasable material, such as chalk. All that now remains is to paint in the colors, and fast-drying, durable acrylic paint is ideal for this purpose. If you feel that additional protection is required, or simply that it would enhance your work, you could then varnish the surface of the motif.

What simpler ways could there be to decorate your home with charming floral flourishes? And once you have been bitten by the découpage or stenciling bug—or both—no surface will be safe from your attentions.

Personal Ornamentation

It is sad that many delightful customs involving flowers have either been forgotten or judged unfashionable, not least the age-old traditions of decorating the hair and body with freshly picked blooms. Although this custom is now rare in the Western world (with the exception of weddings, when brides and bridesmaids often wear flowers in their hair and the male participants sport floral boutonnières), it survives in societies that have clung to their indigenous cultural identity. In his paintings of the South Sea's young girls of Tahiti, for example, the French artist Paul Gauguin (1848–1903) featured the exotic blooms worn by his subjects. Visitors to Hawaii are still garlanded with floral lei by young women wearing flowers in their hair, an adornment also used across the Indian

Below: The water gardens (which he called his "outdoor studios") that the French Impressionist painter Claude Monet (1840–1926) created at his home in Giverny inspired the artist's celebrated series of water-lily paintings, collectively called Les Nymphéas.

Above: *An elegant bridal bouquet featuring white roses, English ivy, and a flow of white and gold ribbon.*

Subcontinent, where the *champak* is often worn. Aung San Suu Kyi, the prodemocracy leader of the opposition to the Burmese military government and winner of the Nobel Peace Prize in 1991, also pins a flower in her hair, as seen in rarely published photographs.

In the West, we retain artificial vestiges of such customs by wearing garments made from floral prints, or hair ornaments and jewelry based on floral designs. It is even possible to buy orchids that have been dipped in liquid gold before being fashioned into pendants, charms, or brooches, yet while their natural forms are retained intact, the process inevitably obscures their exquisite coloring and softness. While such artifice has its place in the vocabulary of floral ornamentation, it may be time to return to nature and rediscover the unrivaled versatility and beauty of the originals.

Perhaps the most elegant way to wear flowers is in a buttonhole, and boutonnières have the advantage of suiting both sexes. Their origins lie in medieval times, when knights would pin their ladies' "favors" to their breasts (double-headed daisies, for example, signifying requited love), but the male fashion of sporting fresh flowers in buttonholes really took off during Victorian times. (Reportedly, the trend was started by Prince Albert, who plucked out a rose from Queen Victoria's wedding bouquet and inserted it into his frock coat as a sign of his love for his new wife.) To this day, roses, carnations, or, indeed, many other types of flowers, are commonly worn by men with their "morning dress" at English weddings, but there is no reason why boutonnières should be reserved for special occasions. You can easily make your own by cutting a flower stem close to the bloom, soaking a small wad of cotton wool in cold water, squeezing out the excess water, and wrapping it around the stem. Finally, either encase the cotton wool in aluminum foil or wrap florist's tape around it before pinning it to your lapel or, if your jacket has one, inserting it into the buttonhole.

Corsages—miniature flower arrangements—also make deliciously fragrant floral accessories for such special occasions as weddings or gala evenings, especially if exotic flowers like orchids are chosen. They are, however, more complicated to fashion than boutonnières because the stems require wiring (and if you are wearing an expensive or favorite outfit, it is vital that you first brush off the pollen so that it does not stain the fabric). If you are interested in making your own corsage, consult a specialist publication for instructions; otherwise, any good florist will make up a corsage for you to order. Fresh, dried, or artificial blooms make original hat trimmings, too—straw hats, for example, can look enchanting when decorated with country-style, summer blooms. They can be as simple or as complex as you like, ranging from a single flower to a garland that encompasses the crown of the hat (but if you are using fresh cut flowers, again, remember to brush off any pollen and ensure that the stems are covered to avoid water seepage). The best way to prepare a fresh flower for millinery use is to wire its stem with florist's wire, which you can also use to stitch it into place; dried and artificial blooms are more easily attached by means of a glue gun.

You might feel daunted by the prospect, and prefer to engage a professional florist, but with a bit of practice you could almost certainly arrange wedding flowers successfully, from bridal and bridesmaids' circlets and headdresses, bouquets, or posies, to flower-embellished pomanders, hoops, or baskets. For less formal occasions, however, you could experiment with any number of other ideas, including attaching flowers to hair combs (they usually need to be wired, prearranged, and then secured to the comb with floral tape zigzagged through the teeth). And what could be simpler than creating a floral choker by sewing Velcro to each end of a velvet ribbon to secure it to the neck and then stitching a dried or fresh bloom to the center with florist's wire? Like generations before them, twenty-first-century children still love to make daisy chains, but why should they have all the fun?

Below: Expertly carved full-blown roses add an air of grandeur and opulence to this handsome table. The stylistic pedigree of the scrollwork foliage that links the centrally placed rose and the table legs dates back to Classical Greece.

The Captivating Forms of Chinoiserie

The floral decoration that has been applied to the Western earthenware vase opposite is inspired by the exquisitely delicate style that originated in China. Chinoiserie became popular during the eighteenth century.

Floral Style *Au Naturel*

The solid bronze goblet pictured below has been engraved with a wealth of graceful flowers, fruits, and foliage in a naturalistic style that is reminiscent of late medieval art. This period had a great influence on the Arts and Crafts movement, beginning in the late nineteenth century.

The Mystical Rose of Heaven   *Page 234*

In his masterpiece *The Virgin of the Rose Garden* (1448), the German painter Stefan Lochner depicted the "Madonna and Child" sheltered by a bower of climbing roses. The white rose symbolizes the Virgin Mary's chaste, spiritual love, and the red rose, Christ's love for humanity.

The Sacred Flower of Enlightenment *Page 235*

A bevy of lotuses adorns this Buddhist mandala, which depicts the Round of Existence in the clutches of Mahakala, the deity of time. Symbolizing perfect enlightenment, the lotus is the most significant flower in Buddhist belief.

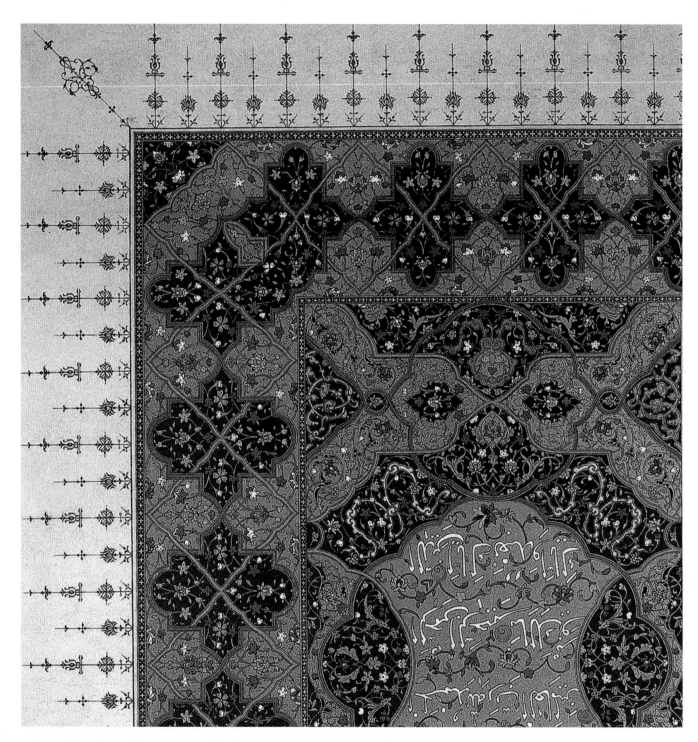

The Floral Arabesques of Islam

These pages from the Qur'an, the sacred book of Islam, are richly decorated with highly stylized floral and foliate motifs in accordance with Islam's prohibition on the figurative depiction of living things. Representing the garden of paradise and the sanctity of nature, such patterns came to be known as "arabesques," or "moresques."

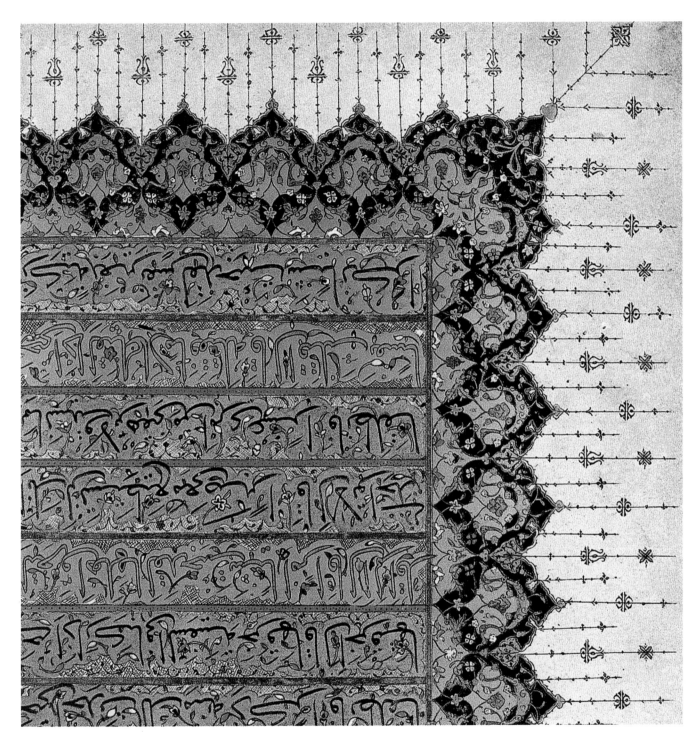

Tributes to Ephemeral Beauty *Overleaf*

Vincent van Gogh's *Sunflowers* (page 238), perhaps the world's best-known flower painting, was created in 1888, the year in which van Gogh was joined in Arles, France, by his fellow artist Paul Gauguin, who captured his colleague at work in *Vincent van Gogh Painting Sunflowers*. The fact that van Gogh immortalized the golden-hued flowers that seem to represent sunny optimism only two years before he committed suicide imbues this masterpiece with great poignancy. Although Gauguin's *Still Life with Mandolin* (page 239) predates his departure for Tahiti in 1891, in the South Seas the artist remained mesmerized by the loveliness of flowers.

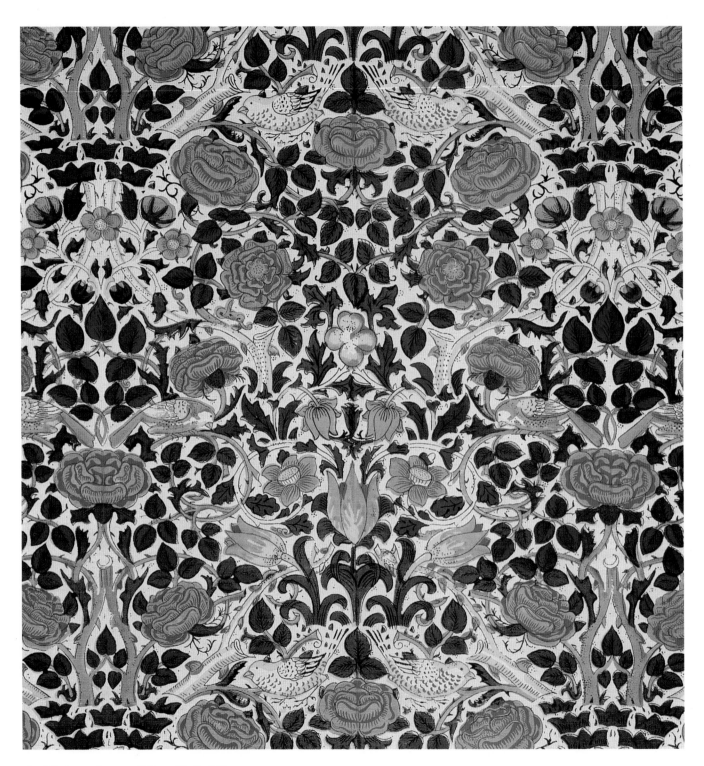

A Champion of English Flora

William Morris's love of flowers inspired both of these textile designs, for which he used vegetable rather than chemical dyes and ignored the cheaper process of roller-printing in favor of block-printing by hand like the artisans of old. Faithful to his ideal of medieval craftsmanship and subject matter, this master artist depicted flowers native to English fields, gardens, and hedgerows, including roses, tulips, carnations, and sunflowers.

Roses and Lilies Transformed *Page 242*

Floral magic has transformed both this ceiling rose and the light fixture suspended from it into magnificent *objets d'art*. The molded-plaster motifs of the ceiling rose are derived from Classical antiquity, while the organic forms of the calla-lily lights with their arrow-shaped leaves are in the style of Art Nouveau.

Classical Detailing *Page 243*

Floral flourishes in the Neoclassical style enrich this handsome stone fireplace surround with carved roses, figs, grapes, and foliage.

Eclectic Elegance

The decoration applied to the substantial fireplace surround above comprises a mixture of styles that is typical of the late nineteenth century. Both Classical and medieval influences can be discerned in the floral motifs of the mantelshelf and fireback.

A Household Devoted to Flowers

The sumptuous interior opposite is a tribute to floral ornament, from the patterned fabric upholstery of the chair in the foreground to the wallpaper frieze along the upper walls and the expensive Oriental rugs.

In the Grand Manner

The intricate molded cornice, decorative plaque, and fire-place entablature opposite form a harmonious exemplar of eighteenth-century interior design. Both the rococo and the Neoclassical styles favored such Classically inspired motifs as the flower-filled vase, shellwork scrolling foliage, and beribboned floral swags seen here.

Embowered in Flowers

Gilt-framed oval mirrors like this example above, with carved floral swags, date back to eighteenth-century France. The wallpaper's roses entwined with garlands were popular with the Victorians, and during that period highly decorative floral patterns were manufactured widely by improved techniques.

Floral Appliqué Works

The extravagant embellishment of this Late Victorian façade (opposite) shows the American penchant for adapting interior decor to exteriors during the exuberant Queen Anne Revival era.

A Symbol of Secrecy

Molded-plaster ceiling roses came into use during the eighteenth century, but they had long served to remind those who held covert meetings ("under the rose"), *sub rosa,* of the need for secrecy.

Arts and Crafts in Bloom

Philip Webb (1831–1915), the architect of William Morris's Red House (1860), designed the rush-seated ebonized armchair, settle, and side chair above, harmoniously grouped with a floral Morris & Co. wallpaper and area rug. The Morris chair opposite, another Webb design, is upholstered in the chintz fabric "Daffodil." English Arts and Crafts architect and designer Arthur Heygate Mackmurdo (1851–1942) designed the fretwork dining chair (1865) at left, with its whiplash curves and organic floral forms.

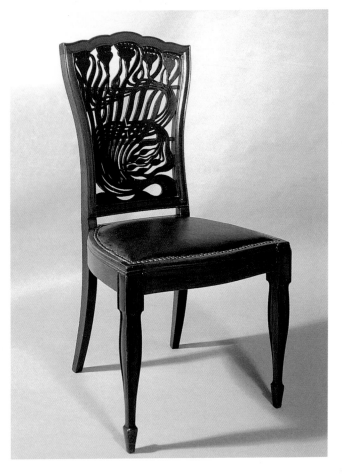

Index

Bibliography

Sandy Barnes, *Decorative Painting: Flowers and Finishes*, Search Press Ltd., Tunbridge Wells, 1998.

Fiona Barnett, *New Ways With Fresh Flowers*, Anness Publishing Limited, London, 1996.

Fiona Barnett and Terence Moore, *The Ultimate Book of Fresh and Dried Flowers*, Lorenz Books, London, 1999.

Penny Black, *The Book of Pot Pourri*, Dorling Kindersley, London, published in association with the National Trust, 1995.

Stephen Blackmore, *Illustrated Guide to Wild Flowers*, Kingfisher Books Ltd., London, 1982.

Andi Clevely, *Geoff Hamilton's Year in Your Garden*, Headline Book Publishing, London, 1999.

Susan Conder, *The Complete Geranium*, Collins & Brown Ltd., London, 1992.

J.C. Cooper (ed.), *Brewer's Book of Myth & Legend*, Helicon Publishing Ltd., Oxford, 1995.

Dawn Cusick, *Dried Flower Crafts*, Sterling Publishing Co., Inc., New York, 1995.

Florence G. Dale and Charles J. Ziga, *A Handbook of Edible Flowers*, Barnes and Noble Books, New York, 1999.

Brian Davis, *Kingfisher Guide to Garden Plants*, Kingfisher Publications plc, London, 2000.

Dee Davis, *Découpage*, Thames and Hudson Ltd., London, 1995.

Alastair Duncan, *Art Nouveau*, Thames and Hudson Ltd., London, 1994.

Helen Exley (Ed.), *Flowers*, Exley Publications, Watford, 1992.

Lance Hattatt, *The Gardening Year*, Parragon, Bath, 1997.

Dr. D. G. Hessayon, *The Flower Arranging Expert*, Transworld Publishers Ltd., London, 1996.

Dr. D. G. Hessayon, *The New Flower Expert*, Transworld Publishers Ltd., London, 1999.

Dr. D. G. Hessayon, *The New Rose Expert*, Transworld Publishers Ltd., London, 1996.

Edward Hyams, *The Story of England's Flora*, Penguin Books Ltd., Harmondsworth, 1979.

Will Ingwersen, *Classic Garden Plants*, The Hamlyn Publishing Group Ltd., Feltham, 1975.

Alison Jenkins, *Pressed Flowers*, Southwater, London, 2000.

Katherine Kear, *Flower Wisdom*, Thorsons, London, 2000.

Richard Marshall and Charles J. Ziga, *A Handbook of Herbs*, Barnes and Noble Books, New York, 1999.

Anne McIntyre, *Flower Power*, Henry Holt and Company, Inc., New York, 1996.

Judith Miller, *The Style Sourcebook*, Stewart, Tabori and Chang, New York, 1998.

Kitty Morse, *Edible Flowers*, Ten Speed Press, Berkeley, 1995.

The National Gallery, *Flowers in Art*, M.Q. Publications Ltd., in association with National Gallery Company Ltd., London, 2000.

Sue Nicholls, *Dried Flowers: A Handbook, A-Z*, Lutterworth Press, Cambridge, 1984.

Linda Parry, *Textiles of the Arts and Crafts Movement*, Thames and Hudson Ltd., London, 1988.

Mragaret Pickston, *The Language of Flowers*, Michael Joseph Ltd., London, 1968.

Jenny Raworth and Susan Berry, *Flower Arranging*, The Reader's Digest Association Limited, London, 1996.

Yvonne Rees, *The Decorative Artist*, Quantum Books Ltd., London, 1988.

Gay Robins, *The Art of Ancient Egypt*, British Museum Press, London, 1997.

The Royal Horticultural Society Plant Guides, *Annuals and Biennials*, Dorling Kindersley, London, 1997.

David Stuart and James Sutherland, *Plants from the Past*, Viking, Harmondsworth, 1987.

David Sutton, *Kingfisher Field Guide to the Wild Flowers of Britain and Northern Europe*, Kingfisher Publications plc, London, 1996.

Diana Wells, *100 Flowers and How They Got Their Names*, Algonquin Books of Chapel Hill, Chapel Hill, 1997.

Acknowledgments and Photo Credits

The publisher would like to thank the following individuals for their help in the preparation of this book: Robin Langley Sommer, editor; Erin Pikor, photo editor; Charles J. Ziga, art director; Nikki L. Fesak, graphic designer; Clare Haworth-Maden, indexer. Grateful acknowledgment is also made to Larry Angier and Carolyn Fox for art direction of the special photography; to Jeffery Jones of The Garden Spot, Jackson, CA; Sandi Trassare of Avenue Florist, Lodi, CA; Lois Billigmeier of Fiore Floral & Gifts, Linden, CA; Cindi Burton; Diane Matich; and to the following individuals and institutions for permission to reproduce illustrations and photographs on the pages listed: Courtesy, **AKG LONDON**: 18, 19, 20, 21, 22, 23, 233, 236, 237; © **Larry Angier**: 170, 171, 178–79, 190, 191, 192, 193, 218, 220, 230; © **Mary Liz Austin**: 52–53, 94, 95, 104, 106, 108, 118, 162-63, 174; © **Ed Cooper**: 26, 72, 92, 105, 110, 111, 124, 129, 132-33, 135, 137, 138, 231, 232; © **Terry Donnelly**: 93, 116, 122-23, 154; © **Carolyn Fox**: 1, 3, 4, 32–33, 41, 82, 98, 144, 146, 147, 156, 158, 166, 176, 177, 178, 180, 180-81, 182, 183, 184-85, 186, 187, 188, 189, 200, 208-09, 210-11, 212, 219, 221, 227, 248; © **Blake Gardner**: 39, 55, 74, 109; © **Rudi Holnsteiner**: 6, 27, 34, 44–45, 48, 86-87, 90, 102, 125, 126, 127, 128, 130, 131, 134, 136, 138-39, 140, 141, 143, 153, 164, 168, 169, 172, 173, 175; © **Wolfgang Kaehler**: 7, 8, 12, 13, 28–29, 30, 35, 36, 37, 42, 46, 47, 54, 60, 67, 85, 148, 150, 160, 167, 196, 215, 222; Courtesy, **William Morris Gallery**, Walthamstow, London: 228, 240, 241, 250, 251; **Planet Art**: 229, 238, 239; © **Paul Rocheleau**: 11, 66, 81, 83, 91, 152, 155, 159, 161, 165, 194, 206, 207, 226, 242, 243, 244, 245, 246, 247, 249; **Saraband Image Library**: 224, 225; © **John Sylvester**: 2, 24, 25, 31, 43, 50, 78, 79, 84, 88, 89, 96-97, 97, 98-99, 100-01, 103; © **Jack Vartoogian**: 223; © **Charles J. Ziga**: 9, 10, 14, 15, 16, 17, 38, 40, 49, 51, 56, 57, 58, 59, 61, 62, 63, 64, 65, 68–69, 70, 71, 75, 76, 77, 80, 107, 112-13, 114, 114-15, 117, 119, 120, 121, 142, 149, 151, 157, 197, 198, 199, 201, 202, 203, 204, 205, 213, 214, 216, 217, 235.